Russia in World History

The New Oxford World History

Russia in World History

Barbara Alpern Engel

Janet Martin

OXFORD

UNIVERSITY PRESS

OXFORD

UNIVERSITY PRESS

Oxford University Press is a department of the University of
Oxford. It furthers the University's objective of excellence in research,
scholarship, and education by publishing worldwide.

Oxford   New York
Auckland   Cape Town   Dar es Salaam   Hong Kong   Karachi
Kuala Lumpur   Madrid   Melbourne   Mexico City   Nairobi
New Delhi   Shanghai   Taipei   Toronto

With offices in
Argentina   Austria   Brazil   Chile   Czech Republic   France   Greece
Guatemala   Hungary   Italy   Japan   Poland   Portugal   Singapore
South Korea   Switzerland   Thailand   Turkey   Ukraine   Vietnam

Oxford is a registered trademark of Oxford University Press
in the UK and certain other countries.

Published in the United States of America by
Oxford University Press
198 Madison Avenue, New York, NY 10016

© Oxford University Press 2015

Library of Congress Cataloging-in-Publication Data
Engel, Barbara Alpern.
Russia in world history / Barbara Alpern Engel and Janet Martin.
pages cm. — (New Oxford world history)
Includes bibliographical references and index.
ISBN 978–0–19–994787–4 (hardback : alkaline paper) —
ISBN 978–0–19–994789–8 (paperback : alkaline paper)   1. Russia—History.
2. Soviet Union—History.   3. Russia (Federation)—History.
4. Russia—Relations.   5. Cultural pluralism—Russia—History.
6. Social change—Russia—History.   I. Martin, Janet, 1945 – II. Title.
DK40.E58 2015
947—dc23
2015001743

1 3 5 7 9 8 6 4 2
Printed inthe United States of America
on acid-free paper

Frontispiece: *Group of Russian peasants posed at an outdoor table.*
Library of Congress, LC-USZ62-43049

Contents

Editors' Preface

This book is part of the New Oxford World History, an innovative series that offers readers an informed, lively, and up-to-date history of the world and its people that represents a significant change from the "old" world history. Only a few years ago, world history generally amounted to a history of the West—Europe and the United States—with small amounts of information from the rest of the world. Some versions of the "old" world history drew attention to every part of the world *except* Europe and the United States. Readers of that kind of world history could get the impression that somehow the rest of the world was made up of exotic people who had strange customs and spoke difficult languages. Still another kind of "old" world history presented the story of areas or peoples of the world by focusing primarily on the achievements of great civilizations. One learned of great buildings, influential world religions, and mighty rulers but little of ordinary people or more general economic and social patterns. Interactions among the world's peoples were often told from only one perspective.

This series tells world history differently. First, it is comprehensive, covering all countries and regions of the world and investigating the total human experience—even those of so-called peoples without histories living far from the great civilizations. "New" world historians thus share in common an interest in all of human history, even going back millions of years before there were written human records. A few "new" world histories even extend their focus to the entire universe, a "big history" perspective that dramatically shifts the beginning of the story back to the big bang. Some see the "new" global framework of world history today as viewing the world from the vantage point of the Moon, as one scholar put it. We agree. But we also want to take a closeup view, analyzing and reconstructing the significant experiences of all of humanity.

This is not to say that everything that has happened everywhere and in all time periods can be recovered or is worth knowing, but that there is much to be gained by considering both the separate and interrelated stories of different societies and cultures. Making these connections is still another crucial ingredient of the "new" world history. It emphasizes connectedness and interactions of all kinds—cultural, economic, political, religious, and social—involving peoples, places, and processes. It makes comparisons and finds similarities. Emphasizing both the comparisons and interactions is critical to developing a global framework that can deepen and broaden historical understanding, whether the focus is on a specific country or region or on the whole world.

The rise of the new world history as a discipline comes at an opportune time. The interest in world history in schools and among the general public is vast. We travel to one another's nations, converse and work with people around the world, and are changed by global events. War and peace affect populations worldwide as do economic conditions and the state of our environment, communications, and health and medicine. The New Oxford World History presents local histories in a global context and gives an overview of world events seen through the eyes of ordinary people. This combination of the local and the global further defines the new world history. Understanding the workings of global and local conditions in the past gives us tools for examining our own world and for envisioning the interconnected future that is in the making.

Bonnie G. Smith
Anand Yang

Preface

On December 25, 1991, Mikhail Gorbachev announced his resignation as president of the Soviet Union. "We are living in a new world," Gorbachev declared. "An end has been put to the Cold War and to the arms race, and the insane militarization of our country."[1] This momentous speech promised an end to hostilities with the United States that had divided "East" from "West" for close to half a century, and terminated the first global experiment with communism.

The speech also heralded the breakup of the fifteen republics that had comprised the Union of Soviet Socialist Republics (USSR), eliminating one of the world's two great superpowers. As the other republics became independent, the Russian Republic ceased to be the dominant component of the USSR and became simply the Russian Federation. The dissolution of the USSR put an end to an empire, the second largest in human history, which had been forged over many centuries and at the cost of countless lives. The Soviet experiment offered a new ideological framework to unify the peoples of the Russian empire. Combined with the use of force to quash assertions of autonomy, it had succeeded in holding its multiethnic population together for seven decades. But like its Russian predecessor as well as other contiguous empires such as the Ottoman and Austro-Hungarian empires that collapsed in the early twentieth century, the Soviet Union ultimately failed to contain the pressures of modern nationalism.

Even today, however, although Russia is smaller than it has been since the seventeenth century, it remains highly diverse ethnically as well as formidable in size, almost twice as large as the continental United States. Now, as Russia seeks to regain its former stature in a rapidly changing world and respond to its diverse peoples' aspirations to live better and enjoy greater rights and autonomy, its past has become freshly relevant—to its leaders, to its citizens, and to those who want to understand this fascinating country and its dramatic history.

This book records the efforts of the peoples of a series of Russian states to eke out livings in harsh environments, organize themselves socially and politically, expand and defend their territories, and recover and rebuild after invasion and political collapse. It also traces Russia's role as a crossroads—of invasion, trade, and the mingling of Europeans and Asians. It begins at least a millennium before the formation of the Soviet Union and the Russian Federation, when some Slavic tribes—sedentary, agricultural people—and their Finnic and Baltic neighbors, recognized a group of Norsemen as their overlords. They were known as the Rus. By the ninth century these peoples had fashioned a political entity also known as Rus and to historians, as Kievan Rus, which survived until the thirteenth century, when it was conquered by the Mongols. Significant portions of its population, dwelling in its southwestern and western regions, thereafter followed their own historical paths, eventually emerging as the modern nations of Ukraine and Belarus.

The northern sectors of Kievan Rus, however, upon emerging from Mongol domination in the fifteenth century, became the core of the Russian states that would form successively over the next centuries: Muscovy, the Russian Empire, the USSR, and the Russian Federation. Their ethnic composition, forms of government, and geographic boundaries have varied. Nevertheless, each of these states belongs to the history of Russia.

All of the Russian states shared essential features and faced common challenges. Geographic location and climate shaped all of them. The peoples who established Kievan Rus settled in a forested zone characterized by a mix of deciduous trees and conifers. Amply supplied with game and other forest products, and with fish from its many lakes and rivers, the region was well suited for the cultivation of some crops, such as flax and hemp. But its poor soils, northern location—at latitudes similar to those of Canada and Alaska—and continental climate led to growing seasons shorter than those in most of the rest of Europe and made production of edible grains difficult. Expansion to the east and north, conducted by Kievan Rus and its successor states, added more mixed forest, taiga (boreal forest and coniferous forest), and tundra but not significant arable acreage.

Expansion to the south into the steppe improved Russia's agricultural potential. The steppe was a zone of open grassland that formed a corridor extending across Inner Asia to the plains of Hungary. For centuries a succession of warrior nomads pastured their herds on the rich steppe grasslands, effectively preventing the Russians from settling in the region. It was not until the sixteenth century that Russian forces were able to subordinate some of the fearsome nomads and gradually annex the steppe. But even after Slavic settlers moved into the area, they had difficulty realizing its agricultural potential. Its location, although farther south than long-standing Russian territories, is as far north as Canada. While its soils are rich, the steppe, which gives way to desert to its south and east, has unreliable rainfall. Geography and climate limited the productivity of agriculture, the occupation of the overwhelming majority of Russia's population for centuries. Frequent crop failures rendered the lives of its peasant farmers precarious.

Early Russian states were disadvantaged in other ways as well. Their territories also lacked important mineral resources and precious metals that contributed to the growth of European states to their west. Although the conquest of Siberia would eventually bring reserves of coal, oil, gas, and other valuable minerals, agriculture provided the primary, albeit meager, economic foundation for Russia and its rulers for centuries. A secondary source of revenue was commerce, but Russia's terrain made both domestic and foreign trade challenging. Distances were vast. Kiev and Vladimir are separated by more than 650 miles, Novgorod and Moscow by more than 330. Roads, where they existed, were poor and turned muddy in the spring. Transport on rivers, navigable in the summer and frozen in the winter, was preferable to overland travel. But Russia's great rivers flowed northward to the White Sea or southward to the land-locked Caspian Sea or to the Black Sea, controlled for centuries by the Byzantine and then the Ottoman Empire. Only in the eighteenth century did Russians gain control over access to the Gulf of Finland, an extension of the Baltic Sea, and also over the northern shore of the Black Sea, facilitating trade with the burgeoning commercial economies of western Europe.

Geography also influenced Russia's political relations with its neighbors. Unprotected by natural barriers, the land mass that made up the successive Russian states left them vulnerable to foreign invasion. In addition to the Mongol conquest of the thirteenth century, Russia came close to being overcome by Sweden and the unified commonwealth of Poland-Lithuania at the end of the sixteenth century, and surrendered to the Germans vast swaths of their western borderlands near the end of World War I. French and German armies in the early nineteenth and mid-twentieth centuries, respectively, made deep and damaging inroads into the country.

But the same factors that enabled foreign armies to advance into Russia allowed its rulers to expand their territories outward. Its princes oversaw the growth of Kievan Rus from small settlements hugging the rivers linking modern Novgorod and Kiev into a sprawling federation of principalities, covering territories of modern Ukraine, Belarus, and northern European Russia. The Romanovs, who ruled the Russian state from the early seventeenth century until 1917, transformed it into the largest land empire in modern history, while their successors, the communists, extended its global reach. The empire, painstakingly constructed and reconstructed over the centuries, came apart following the dissolution of the Communist Party in 1991.

Chronic difficulties associated with transportation, communication, and governing the diverse peoples of this enormous landmass created challenges for its rulers, and, ultimately, contributed to an emphasis on powerful, centralized leadership. Successful rulers employed the power of the state not only to defend and expand their domains but also to harness social and economic resources, often at the cost of heavy economic burdens and individual freedom. The reign of Peter the Great was pivotal in this sense. Intensifying changes already under way, Peter oversaw a significant increase in Russia's involvement in European affairs and its emergence as an imperial power, framing Russia's place in the world for the next two centuries. The substantial role of the state means that rulers occupy a prominent place in the story. But so, too, do the subjects who benefited or suffered from their decisions.

One major consequence of Russia's pattern of expansion and contraction is that to be "Russian" has meant different things over the ages. In one sense "Russian" refers to the Russian people, one branch of the family of Eastern Slavs that also includes Ukrainians and Belarusians. But the term is also used to refer collectively to the entire population of the Russian states. To the Slavs, Finns, and Balts of Kievan Rus, Muscovy added the populations dwelling along the Volga River, on the steppe, and in Siberia. The cultures of the Muslim, Turkic-speaking peoples and of the animist herdsmen and hunters of Siberia contrasted sharply with that of sedentary Christian Slavs. Subsequently, the peoples of eastern Poland, including more than 100,000 Jews, of the Baltic region, the Caucasus, Transcaucasia, and Central Asia, all espousing different faiths, speaking different languages, and pursuing distinctive ways of life, supplemented the core population of Slavic peasants, united by their Orthodox Christian faith. By the twentieth century the diversity of the USSR was such that it consisted of more than 120 officially recognized peoples; Russians made up just over one-half of the entire population. The history of Russia is necessarily also a story of efforts to meld a multiethnic polity into a coherent political entity and, to the extent possible to document in so short a book, of the impact of these efforts on its various peoples.

This story is, at the same time, a history of Russia in the world. Russia's successes in overcoming its many disadvantages rested in part on its ability to draw on the cultures and technologies of its neighbors and adapt them to its own circumstances. In turn, the innovations of Russia's peoples spread beyond its borders. The literary achievements of writers such as Leo Tolstoy, Feodor Dostoevsky, and Anton Chekhov; the musical compositions of Igor Stravinsky; the innovative dance and staging of Sergei Dyaghilev's Ballets Russes, to cite only some of the most well-known examples, influenced world culture. In the second half of the twentieth century, the Leninist-Stalinist adaptation of Marxism became a template for socialist states everywhere, helping to divide the world in two. The Christian anarchism of Leo Tolstoy, as articulated in his writings on civil disobedience and non-violence, profoundly affected the worldview of Mahatma Gandhi, and in turn of others who have chosen the same path, including Martin Luther King Jr. and non-violent activists worldwide. Adaptation and innovation continue to drive Russia's development and there is every reason to believe will do so into the future.

A Note on Dates and Names

At the dawn of the eighteenth century, Peter the Great altered the Russian calendar to conform to the Julian calendar, then in use in much of the Western world. Its dates are usually thirteen or fourteen days earlier than the same dates of the Gregorian calendar now in use in the modern West, and adopted by Russia in 1918.

For the names of people and places well known to English readers, we use the form that will be most familiar to them. We have left other names in the transliterated Russian form.

CHAPTER 1

The Formation of Russia

Slavs, Vikings, and Byzantium

Two centuries after the events they reported, the composers of the *Primary Chronicle* or *Tale of Bygone Years* described the formation of Kievan Rus, the earliest forerunner of modern Russia, and its disparate features: a population of Slavic, Finnic, and Baltic tribes; a ruling dynasty descended from a Scandinavian Viking; and an official religion, Christianity, borrowed from Byzantium. Piecing together bits of fact and legend, the chroniclers recorded that in the year 859 CE, "Varangians from beyond the sea imposed tribute" on a group of Finnic and Slavic tribes. Within just a few years, however, "the tributaries of the Varangians" rebelled and "drove [the Varangians] back beyond the sea." But, the tale continued, the tribesmen's efforts "to govern themselves" failed. "There was no law among them, but tribe rose against tribe.... They said to themselves: 'Let us seek a prince who may rule over us and judge us according to the Law.' They accordingly went overseas to the Varangian Russes ... [and] selected three brothers.... [After two years] the oldest, Ryurik ... assumed the sole authority."[1]

The *Primary Chronicle* goes on to describe members of Ryurik's clan extending their authority over a narrow belt of territory hugging the waterways connecting Lake Ladoga and Novgorod in the north to Kiev (modern Kyiv) on the mid-Dnieper River in the south. Intermarrying, trading, and fighting with the monarchs of Europe, the Byzantine Empire, and the Turkic nomads of the steppe to their south, their descendants forged Kievan Rus, a powerful federation of principalities that stretched to Poland and Hungary in the west, the juncture of the Volga and Oka Rivers in the east, and beyond the Sukhona River in the north and survived until the Mongol invasion of the mid-thirteenth century.

The tribes identified by the chroniclers had dwelled in the lands that would become Kievan Rus long before the arrival of the Vikings they called Varangians. The Finns who inhabited the area near Lake Ladoga and along the upper Volga River were members of a larger Finno-Ugrian population that, as early as the fifth to seventh centuries, had occupied lands along the rivers that cut across the northern expanse between Scandinavia and the Ural Mountains. Balts too, although not mentioned in the chronicle report, had settled along the Volkhov, West Dvina, and the upper Volga Rivers.

Slavic tribes had reached the territories of the Finns and Balts in the eighth century. Scholars have theorized that the Slavs began a mass migration from the region north of the Carpathian Mountains in the sixth century. As they dispersed, one group, later known as East Slavs, made their way into the southern forest and forest-steppe zones of modern Ukraine and Belarus. Although these marshes and forests had previously been inhabited, there is no consensus on the identity of their residents before small groups of Slavs, typically kinsmen, settled in scattered locations near major waterways. They constructed log dwellings, each large enough for four or five people and distinguished by their sunken floors and stone hearths, and buried the cremated remains of their dead. Simple handmade pottery vessels, utilitarian tools, and few signs of weapons or fortifications also marked their early settlements.

The Slavs, like the Finns and Balts, fished; hunted game for meat and fur; gathered fruits, berries, nuts, mushrooms, and honey in the forests; raised livestock; and cultivated crops of cereal grains, peas, lentils, flax, and hemp in forest clearings. As soils were exhausted, the farmers cleared new fields using a slash-and-burn method and, when necessary, created new settlements. In pursuit of new agricultural plots and for other, unknown reasons, some tribes moved to the north; others remained on the mid-Dnieper River, near Kiev, or crossed the Dnieper and made their way to the northeast toward the Oka River.

The territories of the Slavs, Finns, and Balts overlapped, but because their populations were small and settlements dispersed they had minimal contact and rarely competed for resources. All three groups as well as the Varangians converged, however, at Old Ladoga (Staraya Ladoga), the first urban settlement established in the northern territories that later became Russia. Located near the mouth of the Volkhov River at Lake Ladoga, Old Ladoga dates to the mid-eighth century. A forge, smith's tools, and artifacts such as boat rivets found at the site of this proto-town suggest that its inhabitants, who are estimated to have grown from a few dozen to several hundred by the mid-ninth century, were craftsmen and that Old Ladoga developed as a transit point for the Vikings who navigated the rivers connecting the Baltic Sea to the Volga River.

Excavations have also revealed that c. 860 Old Ladoga burned. Although the settlement was built of wood and subject to fire, this set of charred remains reflects an unusual conflagration that may be physical evidence of the turmoil that, according to the chronicle, preceded Ryurik's arrival.

Scholars, combining evidence from the chronicle and other written and archaeological sources, have pieced together a more complete account of the founding of Kievan Rus. Vikings, known as both Varangians and Rus, appeared in the eighth century among Slav, Finn, and Balt communities. Explorers and military adventurers, they traded with local inhabitants but also raided villages, took captives, and seized booty. As they sailed eastward to the mid-Volga, they discovered the market center of Bulgar, where they sold their captives and other wares. In exchange they received Islamic silver coins and Asian luxury products, which they took back to Sweden. The lure of silver enticed them to return in greater numbers. By the ninth century, as the chronicle tale reflects, bands of Vikings established permanent residences and more stable relations with the local populations, who became their tributaries and also provided support services for their journeys along the lengthy river routes. Ibn Fadlan, a member of a mission sent by the Caliph of Baghdad to Bulgar in 922, witnessed the Rus praying to their gods for good customers who would buy their slaves and fur pelts for silver. The value they placed on silver was evident in the "rings of gold and silver" worn by their wives. "The man, if he possesses ten thousand *dirhams* [Islamic silver coins], has a neck ring made for his wife," Ibn Fadlan observed. "If he has twenty thousand in his possession, then he has two neck rings made for her. And so his wife receives another neck ring with the addition of each ten thousand *dirhams*. Accordingly it often happens that there are a number of neck rings upon the neck of one of them."[2]

From their base in the region of Ladoga Rus warlords also made their way south. They compelled the Slavic tribes all the way to Kiev to pay tribute and conducted expeditions to Itil, the capital of the Khazar empire, near the mouth of the Caspian Sea. They also ventured toward the Black Sea. In 904–907, according to the *Primary Chronicle*, Oleg, a member of Ryurik's retinue who had displaced the Khazars as overlord of the Slav settlements on the mid-Dnieper, attacked Constantinople and won permission to visit Constantinople on a regular basis to sell goods at the city's markets. This opened a new, long-distance commercial river route connecting the Varangians near the Baltic Sea to the Greeks at Constantinople. Thereafter, every November, in preparation for their annual commercial expedition, the Rus chiefs and their retainers made their rounds among the Slav tribes, collecting tribute. Then, according to the tenth-century Byzantine emperor Constantine VII Porphyrogenitus, in "April, when the ice of the Dnieper river melt[ed], they [came] back to Kiev," where they picked up river boats Slavs had constructed during the winter, and furnished them "with oars and rowlocks and other tackle ... and in the month of June they move[d] off down the river Dnieper" and sailed to Constantinople.[3]

Their journey down the Dnieper River took the Rus hundreds of miles across the steppe south to the Black Sea. Although the steppe contained rich black soils, the Slavs, having only light wooden plows at their disposal, were unable to cultivate it and had not tried to occupy it. For centuries before the Slavs settled in the forests to its north, moreover, the grasslands had been home to nomadic peoples who had successively pushed westward from Central Asia. Among them were the Scythians, known to Herodotus as fierce warriors, who left traces of their presence in the region north of the Black Sea and of their hunting skills in the form of their golden "animal style" artwork. In the late fourth century, following the Scythians and a series of other peoples, the Huns dominated the steppe before gradually proceeding further west, where one of their leaders Atilla famously harassed the frontiers of the Roman Empire. In the sixth century the Avars dominated the region. Some scholars have concluded that their advance further westward sparked the dispersal of the Slavs, including those who reached the mid-Dnieper, from their population centers north of the Carpathian Mountains.

By the ninth and tenth centuries, as Kievan Rus was forming, the Pechenegs displaced the Magyars, ancestors of the Hungarians, and dominated the steppe between the Don and the Danube Rivers. Their control of the pasturelands constituted an additional, powerful incentive for the Slavs to remain within the forests and marshes, which afforded some protection from the nomads' intermittent raids on their frontier settlements and seizures of captives, whom they held for ransom or sold as slaves at the Khazar and Byzantine markets. Pecheneg attacks continued until 1036, when Yaroslav the Wise broke their siege of Kiev and soundly defeated them.

The Qïpchaqs, also known as Polovtsy and Cumans, who succeeded the Pechenegs as masters of the steppe, constituted an even more ferocious threat. Their first raid, launched in 1061, broke through Rus defenses that had contained the Pechenegs, and their campaign in 1096 reached Kiev. The chronicler, a terrified eyewitness, reported, "The Polovcians almost entered the city [Kiev], burned the suburbs about the town, and then attacked ... the Crypt Monastery while we were resting in our cells after matins, and they howled about the monastery.... [W]e fled, some of us behind the building of the monastery, and others to its various rooms. [They] ... slew the brethren in the monastery and wandered about among the cells, breaking down the doors, and they carried off whatever they could find in the various rooms."[4]

But relations between the Rus and the steppe nomads were not exclusively hostile. Emperor Constantine noted the strong incentives the Rus had to maintain peaceful relations with the Pechenegs. If they did not, the nomads would attack their towns while the the Rus were away conducting wars. They were also vulnerable when they traveled to the "imperial city of the Romans [i.e., Constantinople], either for war or for trade." The emperor explained: "when the Rus come with their ships to the barrages [rapids] of the [Dnieper] river[, they] ... cannot pass through unless they lift their ships off the river and carry them past by portaging them on their shoulders." The Pechenegs would then "set upon them, and, as they [the Rus] cannot do two things at once, they are easily routed and cut to pieces."[5] To prevent such attacks the Rus thus sought peace with the Pechenegs and, at times, formed alliances with them, as they would later with the Qïpchaqs. They also traded with the nomads, bartering grain and textiles for their cattle, sheep, and especially horses, which the Rus, who were abandoning the use of foot soldiers to better fight their new foes, used as mounts for their own warriors.

A more formal political structure gradually emerged from the rudimentary relations among the Rus, Slavs, Finns, and Balts, based on tribute collection, protection, and trade. The descendants of Ryurik, later referred to as the Ryurikid dynasty, became princes, ruling over a predominantly Slavic society melded from the tributary tribes. Initially tribal leaders were responsible for collecting and delivering tribute, supporting the Rus during their rounds, and supervising the construction of river boats. But in 945, after Igor forcibly extracted additional tribute payments from the Derevlyane, the Slavic tribe dwelling on the Pripyat River, the tribesmen murdered him. According to a tale, replete with elements of folklore, recorded in the *Primary Chronicle*, Igor's widow Olga took revenge, cunningly entrapping and executing tribal emissaries and leaders. Finally, using trickery, she burned their main town, killed many of its inhabitants, reduced others to slavery, and imposed harsh tribute on the remainder. Afterward, she appointed her own agents to oversee functions previously handled by tribal leaders.

Olga's grandson Vladimir developed the structure further, establishing two distinguishing and enduring features of Kievan Rus. In 978–980, while preparing to seize Kiev from his brother, Vladimir sought assistance from a Varangian chief, unrelated to Ryurik's clan, who controlled the region of Polotsk. When the chief refused, Vladimir killed him, married his daughter, and established exclusive Ryurikid control over the Rus lands.

His second great accomplishment was the adoption of Christianity. Once in power in Kiev, Vladimir determined to reinforce his political position by creating religious unity among his diverse subjects. Initially, he established a single pantheon, which included Norse, Slav, Finn, and Iranian gods worshipped by the various peoples of his realm. But he was also intrigued by the monotheistic religions of his neighbors: Judaism of the Khazars, Islam of the Bulgars on the Volga, and Christianity of the Europeans and the Byzantines. The chronicle account portrays him sending envoys to each of them to observe their religious practices. Disappointed with Judaism and Islam, his agents enthusiastically reported on their visit to Constantinople: "the Greeks led us to the edifices where they worship their God, and we knew not whether we were in heaven or on earth.... We know only that God dwells there among men, and their service is fairer than the ceremonies of other nations." In 988, Vladimir gave up his many wives and concubines, personally accepted baptism, and married Anna, sister of the Byzantine emperor. Directing that the idols of the previously recognized gods "be cut to pieces ... [or] burned with fire," he ordered the inhabitants of Kiev to be baptized in the Dnieper river and "founded the Church of St. Basil on the hill where the idol[s] ... had been set, and where the prince and the people had offered their sacrifices."[6] The patriarch of Constantinople appointed a metropolitan, the chief prelate for Kiev and all Rus, and Vladimir sent bishops and priests, accompanied by his sons, to establish and defend Christianity as the official religion throughout his realm.

For converting his realm to Christianity, the Russian Orthodox Church later recognized Vladimir as a saint. But not all members of the population of Kievan Rus welcomed the new religion. In Novgorod, which had replaced Old Ladoga as the main town in northwestern Rus, residents rebelled when the recently arrived Christian bishop ordered the idol of the god Perun thrown in the Volkhov River. To the representatives of the Church, the customs of some of the Slav tribes seemed vile. The monks who compiled the *Primary Chronicle* contemptuously described pre-Christian Slavs as living "like cattle. They killed one another, ate every impure thing, and there was no marriage among them, but instead they seized upon maidens by capture."[7] Both Vladimir and his son Yaroslav issued statutes that placed marriage as well as a range of other social and civil matters, including burial rites; "divorce; fornication; adultery; rape; ... witchcraft; sorcery; [and] magic" under the jurisdiction of the Church, which then pressured the populace to adopt its rules and rituals.[8] But even as some women began to wear pendants with the Christian cross, many, clinging to their traditional religious beliefs, continued to rely on amulets with pagan symbols to ward off evil spirits well into the twelfth century.

The community of Christian nations, however, rapidly embraced Kievan Rus. Vladimir's sons and grandchildren married members of royal families throughout Europe. His son Yaroslav married Irina (Ingegerd), the daughter of Olaf, the first Christian king of Sweden. One of Yaroslav's sons wed the sister of the king of Poland, which had also adopted Christianity in the tenth century. Another married the sister of the bishop of Trier, while the wife of a third came from the Byzantine imperial family. But it was the marriages of Yaroslav's daughters that displayed Kievan Rus's wide range of connections. One married the king of Norway, and then, after being widowed, the king of Denmark. Another married the king of France and, after his death, served as regent for her son. A third wed the king of Hungary and a fourth, genealogical evidence suggests, married into the royal house of England. Members of later generations continued to wed members of the royal houses of central and northern Europe.

The adoption of Christianity also opened Kievan Rus to Byzantine cultural influences and broadened commercial ties between the two societies. Byzantine architectural styles became the model for new buildings in Kiev. Greek design was evident in the Church of the Holy Virgin, also called the Church of the Tithe to commemorate Vladimir's endowment of one-tenth of his revenues to the Church. Set on the site of a pagan cemetery and constructed of brick and stone, it was completed in 996. Along with two other palatial structures it formed the centerpiece of the newly fortified sector of the town known as "Vladimir's city." The Cathedral of St. Sophia, which became the seat of the metropolitan and the symbolic center of Christian Rus, was built during Yaroslav's reign. Cathedrals erected during the 1030s–60s notably in Chernigov (Chernihiv), located east of the Dnieper River, and in

Novgorod signaled the entrenchment of Christianity and the transmission of Byzantine architectural styles beyond Kiev.

The construction projects brought master craftsmen with their technologies and skills from various parts of the Byzantine Empire to Kievan Rus. Using Byzantine designs and imported building materials, including marble and glazed tiles, they trained local apprentices and workmen as they erected the new cathedrals and adorned their interiors with frescoes, mosaics, and silver-framed icons. Clergymen from Constantinople and other Christian centers also promoted literacy and the production of written documents. Scandinavian runes on coins, amulets, and other objects as well as inscriptions on Islamic *dirhams* reveal that the concept of writing was known to the Slavic and Finnic populations in the pre-Christian era. But there is little evidence that they used written language themselves before churchmen brought to Kievan Rus ecclesiastical texts, translated from Greek into Church Slavonic, which was written in Cyrillic, an alphabet named after St. Cyril and derived from Greek. Ecclesiastical bookmen distributed copies of the texts among the new churches and monasteries and, using Church Slavonic, which became the literary language of Kievan Rus, translated more texts and also produced new chronicles, sermons, and stories of saints' lives. Monks of the Pechersky Monastery, founded in the mid-eleventh century outside Kiev and known also as the Crypt Monastery or the Monastery of the Caves, composed the *Primary Chronicle* or *Tale of Bygone Years,* an annalistic account of historical events, princely records, and legends that narrates the entrance of Kievan Rus into the Christian world and its progressive development. Its extant versions, preserved as the initial sections of two later (fourteenth- and fifteenth-century) chronicles, and another chronicle composed in Novgorod constitute the earliest written accounts of the history of Kievan Rus.

Written records were less common in princely courts; their official documents have survived only in summaries entered into the chronicles or in copies made centuries after the purported originals had been generated. The *Primary Chronicle* nevertheless reports that Vladimir "took the children of the best families, and sent them to schools for instruction in book-learning." And for purposes of religious education Yaroslav "applied himself to books, and read them continually day and night."[9] His daughter Anna, whose husband Henry I of France and son were illiterate, signed official documents for them. The populace of Kievan Rus also gradually embraced the technology of writing,

In the early twelfth century, Gyurgii, a man identified only by his first name, wrote to his parents urging them to sell their residence in Novgorod and go to Smolensk or Kiev, where food was cheaper, or, at least, send word to him that they were alive and well. Although it is not known how widely literacy spread in Kievan Rus, messages such as Gyurgii's indicate that people or the scribes they hired commonly sent written notes etched onto the interior of readily available pieces of birch bark to communicate with family members and associates about their personal affairs and everyday activities. Courtesy of V. L. Yanin.

as revealed by the many notes on birchbark fragments excavated by archaeologists in Novgorod and other towns.

Yaroslav and his descendants also introduced law codes for Kievan Rus society. The first, known as the *Russkaya Pravda*, focused on crimes, such as murder, assault, and robbery, rather than civil matters, and was based on customary law. But even as it recognized vengeance justice for homicides and other crimes, it set limits, defining which family members could avenge a homicide victim, when eyewitnesses were required to corroborate an accusation, and, evidently to circumvent endless feuds, when contending parties should end their disputes. An expanded version of the *Russkaya Pravda*, produced in the twelfth century, substituted monetary compensation for vengeance and prescribed the fines for different off--enses. The varying size of the fines reflected the hierarchical social order emerging in Kievan Rus. Compensation for the deaths of persons employed by princes was higher than for commoners, that for skilled craftsmen higher than for peasants and slaves, and that for men higher than for women. But princely involvement was minimal. Neither the *Russkaya Pravda* nor its expanded version mentioned judges or a princely court system.

The position of prince of Kiev was at the peak of the hierarchy glimpsed in the law code. But both Vladimir and Yaroslav attained that position only after fighting their brothers. Hoping to avoid similar succession struggles, Yaroslav admonished his sons: "love one another, since ye are brothers by one father and mother. If ye abide in amity with one another, God will dwell among you, and will subject your enemies to you, and ye will live in peace. But if ye dwell in envy and dissension, quarreling with one another, then ye will perish yourselves and bring to ruin the land of your ancestors." On the eve of his death he divided his realm among his sons, bequeathing Kiev to the eldest, and directing the others to "heed him as ye have heeded me, that he may take my place among you."[10]

Scholars have interpreted Yaroslav's testament to his sons as a basis for establishing an order of succession. According to the new system, the eldest member of the eldest generation of the dynasty would be the senior or grand prince of the realm and rule Kiev. Younger brothers followed by members of the next generation, all ranked by seniority, would rule secondary princely seats and rotate into higher posts as they became vacant. At the end of the eleventh century the Ryurikids modified this arrangement. Each princely center and its surrounding territory became the permanent domain of its current prince and his direct descendants. There were two exceptions: Kiev, which continued to be the seat of the senior prince of the entire dynasty, and Novgorod, which from the 1130s selected its own ruler. Novgorodian mayors and other officials, the local elite called boyars, the archbishop (also chosen by the townsmen), and free townsmen exercised more influence over their affairs than their counterparts did in other Rus towns. These exceptions notwithstanding, Kievan Rus became a federation of principalities, often competitive and quarrelsome but bound together by a common dynasty and Church.

Within this framework Kievan Rus flourished. Viking expeditions for raiding and trading had evolved into well-established commercial exchanges among the various centers within Kievan Rus and with their neighbors. Already known during Vladimir's era for its forty churches and eight marketplaces, Kiev was described in the eleventh century as "the largest city of Russia . . . , rival of the scepter of Constantinople, the brightest ornament of Greece."[11] It became not only the political and ecclesiastical capital, but an artisanal and commercial center as well with a population of princes and priests, artisans and traders, soldiers and slaves numbering, by the end of the twelfth century, 36,000 to 50,000 persons. Novgorod also became a prominent commercial center, exporting honey, wax, and fur pelts to Scandinavian and German merchants. Its population grew to 20,000 to 30,000 inhabitants. They dwelled in one- and two-story houses, built of pine logs and set within fenced yards lining intersecting streets, also paved with split logs. During the twelfth century other principalities similarly prospered, enabling their princes to achieve political and military prominence. They included not only the already prominent principality of Chernigov but also the emergent principalities of Smolensk, located between Novgorod and Kiev, Suzdalia on the northeastern Rus frontier, and Volhynia and Galicia west of the Dnieper, all also strategically located on commercial routes.

Despite the growth and vitality of Kievan Rus, living conditions for most of the population were harsh and precarious. In contrast to the princes, their military retainers, merchants, artisans, and clergy who were concentrated in towns, most members of Kievan Rus society were free peasants, that is, agriculturalists. Living in villages, they eked out subsistence livings by cultivating the poor soils, hunting and gathering mushrooms and berries in the forests, and fishing the lakes and rivers. The short growing seasons and frequent natural catastrophes—such as fires, severe storms, floods, early frosts, epidemics, and diseases that attacked their livestock—all made survival precarious. On occasion, crop failures resulted in food shortages for townsmen as well as villagers. Novgorodian chroniclers reported that in 1128 famine conditions were so severe that "the people ate lime leaves, birch bark, pounded wood pulp mixed with husks and straw ... buttercups, moss, [and] horse flesh; and thus many dropp[ed] down from hunger, their corpses were in the streets, in the market place, and on the roads, and everywhere."[12]

Revenues from peasants and townsmen, coupled with booty from their own military campaigns, nevertheless sustained the Ryurikid princes. At the height of the dynasty's collective power each of its branches managed its own affairs, collected its own taxes, maintained its own military retainers, and designed and carried out its own policies toward its immediate neighbors. But they also all continued to recognize Kiev as the center of their common realm and the rightful seat of the senior prince. This arrangement was functional in an expanding realm with a growing number of princes and only rudimentary means of communication and transportation. While leaving the princes to manage their own affairs, it also enabled them in extraordinary circumstances to join forces for a common cause, as they did in 1103 to retaliate against Qïpchaqs for their damaging attack on Kiev; the stunning Rus victory killed twenty Qïpchaq chiefs and brought relative stability to the steppe frontier.

The balance between unity and diffusion of power was delicate. Just as architectural design and artistic styles gave visual representation to the political, ecclesiastical, and commercial dependence of the peripheral principalities on the center, so they also illustrated increasing diversity among the components of the federation from each other and from their center. Cultural achievements in Vladimir, in particular, also displayed the tensions between this emerging center of

Suzdalia and Kiev. Vladimir's Cathedral of the Dormition, constructed in 1158–60, reflected some of the Byzantine influences that were manifest in Kievan buildings. But its white stone walls and decorative bands of arcading marked a distinctive regional variation from the Kievan edifaces. The town also boasted walled fortifications with its own set of Golden Gates, modeled after and rivaling Kiev's. The relocation of the miracle-working Byzantine icon of the "Vladimir" Mother of God, from a suburb of Kiev to Vladimir, also came to symbolize the shifting balance of power in Kievan Rus.

The efforts of the princes of Vladimir-Suzdal as well as those of others to enhance their own principalities led, despite Yaroslav's admonition to his sons, to repeated and ever intensifying conflicts among his heirs. Due to its commercial wealth and political flexibility, Novgorod became one point of contention among the competing princes. The main object of their conflicts, however, was Kiev. By the mid-twelfth century the succession system adopted a century earlier was being contested with frequency and ferocity. Members of the younger generation of princes sought to bypass their elders and thus overturn the principle

The early twelfth-century Greek "Our Lady of Vladimir" icon, which exemplifies a Byzantine "tender" style (Eleusa in Greek, umilenie in Russian) of portraying the Virgin Mother and Child, was removed from a suburb of Kiev in 1155 and taken to Vladimir. Housed by Prince Andrei Bogolyubsky in the Cathedral of the Dormition (Cathedral of the Assumption of the Virgin), it was deeply venerated and came to be regarded as a miraculous protector of Vladimir and later, after its transfer there, of Moscow. By permission of the State Tretyakov Gallery, Moscow, Russia.

of seniority guiding succession to Kiev. When the succession to the Kievan throne once again jumped prematurely to the next generation, Andrei Bogolyubsky of Vladimir organized a coalition of princes that restored the throne for his generation. But in 1169, during that conflict as well as during two subsequent succession struggles, Kiev was sacked, reflecting its diminishing status and the shift in the balance of power between the center and the periphery of Kievan Rus.

The internal conflicts made the lands of Rus vulnerable to external enemies. Hungary and Poland repeatedly threatened the southwestern principalities of Galicia and Volhynia. Lithuanians and the merged Orders of Livonian and Teutonic knights pressured the western Rus principalities, including Novgorod and Smolensk. It was, however, a new menace from the steppe that destroyed the already divided realm of Kievan Rus.

CHAPTER 2

The Formation and Development of Muscovy (1240–1462)

In 1223, a Qïpchaq chief appealed to his son-in-law, the Rus grand prince Mstislav Romanovich, for aid against the aggression of an unknown group of warriors who had appeared on the steppe. At the subsequent battle near the Kalka River these strangers defeated the joint Rus-Qïpchaq forces, leaving at least six Rus princes dead and capturing and later executing Mstislav Romanovich and two other princes. They then disappeared from the steppe just as mysteriously as they had appeared. The bewildered chronicler commented, "we know not whence they came, nor where they hid themselves again; God knows whence He fetched them against us for our sins."[1]

These new adversaries were the Mongols. They represented the Mongol Empire—founded by Temüjin, better known as Chinggis Khan or "emperor of the world"—that stretched from Mongolia to northern China and westward across Central Asia and to eastern Iran. When Chinggis Khan died in 1227, his domain had been apportioned among his four principal sons. While the third son, Ögödei, succeeded his father as great khan, the eldest, Juchi (Jochi), received the westernmost portion (ulus) of the empire, including western Siberia, the Qïpchaq (Polovtsian, Cuman) steppe, and adjacent lands not yet conquered. But Juchi died before his father, leaving his son Batu to lead the military campaigns to realize his inheritance. His portion of the empire would become known as Juchi's ulus, the Qïpchaq khanate, and, more commonly, the Golden Horde.

The Mongol forces returned in 1237. Unlike the earlier force, which had been reconnoitering, this was an army bent on conquest. With Mongol warriors as well as others drafted from previously conquered Turkic-speaking tribesmen from the steppe, often collectively called

Tatars, Batu began his campaigns against the Rus with the destruction of Ryazan, located south of the Oka River. He then attacked Vladimir, the chief town of the northeastern Rus lands. Using battering rams and catapults, his forces, as recorded in the chronicles, "broke the wall down at the Golden Gate ... and they destroyed the whole fortress from all sides, and entered it like demons."[2] After defeating Prince Yurii Vsevolodich of Vladimir and his allies in a battle on the Sit River in February 1238, Batu pressed westward. But spring thaws and muddy roads halted the advance of the Mongol horsemen and spared Novgorod. After subduing the Qïpchaqs and gaining control of the steppe, the Mongols turned their attention back to the Rus in 1239–40. Their campaigns culminated in an assault on Kiev. One chronicle account described their assault on the city's walls and entrance into the Kievan Rus capital. Within the city "there could be seen and heard the clashing of lances and clanging of shields, and the arrows flew so thickly that one could not see the sky. It was dark because of the multitude of Tatar arrows, and the dead lay everywhere, and everywhere blood flowed like water.... The people ... fled into the church choirloft with their goods, and from their weight the church walls collapsed; and so the Tatars took Kiev on the sixth day of the month of December [1240]."[3]

While the Mongols then overwhelmed the southwestern Rus principalities and invaded Poland and Hungary, the defeated population of Kievan Rus struggled with the effects of the onslaught. Few members of the princely stratum and military elite remained. At the Battle on the Sit alone Yurii Vsevolodich, three of his sons, and two of his nephews along with many of their military retainers had been killed. The surviving princes nonetheless rallied to prevent attacks on their newly vulnerable western frontiers. In 1239, barely a year after the attack on Vladimir, Yurii's brother and successor, Prince Yaroslav Vsevolodich, managed to fend off incursions by the Lithuanians, who were in the early stages of fashioning a new state that in the fourteenth century would absorb western portions of Kievan Rus. His son Alexander, as prince of Novgorod, repeatedly defended that region from Swedes and Livonian knights. After his victory over the former at the Neva River in 1240, he was known as Alexander Nevsky.

The Mongols' devastating attacks affected townsmen and villagers as well. Although some of the Kievan Rus towns, such as Novgorod, remained intact, two-thirds of them, according to estimates based on archaeological evidence, had suffered the same fate as Kiev and Vladimir. Almost 20 percent never recovered. Many peasant villages, looted and burned by the invaders, were abandoned by their inhabitants, who fled to the safety of surrounding forests or towns that had escaped damage. The Mongols, however, killed and captured so many townsmen and peasants, men and women, princes and commoners that they reduced the population by, possibly, 10 percent.

Batu and his armies ended their military campaigns in 1242, when word reached them that Great Khan Ögödei had died. Batu then retreated to the steppe north of the Black Sea. While many of his chieftains joined other Mongols from all parts of the empire near Qaraqorum, the imperial capital built in 1235, to select Ögödei's successor, Batu began to consolidate his control over his domain. He distributed grazing lands to his nomadic followers; constructed Sarai, his new capital city, on the lower Volga; and imposed a new political order on the Rus principalities.

From his new headquarters Batu required the surviving Rus princes to appear before him to receive patents (*yarlyki*), granting them permission to remain as local rulers of their ancestral domains. When Mikhail, prince of the southern principality of Chernigov, offended the khan during his visit, however, he was executed. Batu thus made it clear that not only the princes' right to rule but their very lives had become dependent on his favor. Just as they allowed the Ryurikid princes to retain their positions, Batu and his successors allowed the Orthodox Church to continue to function and even established a diocese at Sarai in 1261.

In addition to their domestic responsibilities, the Mongols obliged the Rus princes to perform exacting and dangerous services for them. Batu ordered Yaroslav of Vladimir to travel thousands of miles to Qaraqorum, where Ögödei's successor Güyüg was being enthroned. Another visitor, John of Plano Carpine, a Franciscan monk and legate of Pope Innocent IV, observed Yaroslav among the attendees assembled from all points of the empire. He also reported that after the khan's mother invited Yaroslav "to eat and drink with her ... [he] was immediately taken ill and died seven days later and his whole body turned bluish-grey in a strange fashion." Carpine added, "This made everybody think that he had been poisoned there."[4] Yaroslav's sons Alexander and Andrei were nonetheless required to make the same arduous journey to the great khan. When they returned in the winter of 1248–49, the anxious princes of Rostov, Yaroslavl, and other towns of Suzdalia, who were assembled in Vladimir, greeted them with relief. Rus princes faced other hazards. Some fell seriously ill and even died while making their required trips to the lower Volga. They were also called upon to participate in the Mongols' military campaigns. But the princes could also secure favor and privilege. Chroniclers report that for their participation in a Mongol campaign in the north Caucasus in 1278, the khans rewarded the Rus princes and sent them home with honor. A few Rus princes, moreover, formed close personal bonds with the Tatars and even married Tatar women.

The Mongols also compelled the Rus princes to aid in the collection of tribute. From the moment of their conquest of each Rus city, from Ryazan to Kiev, the Mongols had demanded "tithes from everyone—from the princes and from all ranks of people. And they also demanded one-tenth of all the horses in the city."[5] In 1257, in accordance with a policy adopted for the entire empire, the Golden Horde khan ordered a census of the northern Rus population. Although the process initially went smoothly, the Novgorodians, aware the census would be used as a basis for assessing tribute and conscripting men, resisted. Two years later the Tatars returned with Prince Alexander Nevsky. Riding through the narrow, wooden streets of the city and "writing down the Christian houses," they left only after they had "numbered them [the Novgorodians] for tribute and taken it."[6] Popular uprisings in Rostov, Yaroslavl, and other northeastern towns drove out the tribute collectors in 1262. Alexander rushed to the horde to prevail upon the khan not to take punitive action. While there, he became ill and died in 1263.

The ongoing Mongol demands for tribute and conscripts as well as punitive expeditions compounded the devastating effects of the initial conquest. Typically, the Mongols obliged conscripts and captives to support their armies or sold them as slaves, sometimes transporting them to distant parts of their vast empire. The Mongols particularly sought skilled craftsmen, who worked for the Mongols in the construction of Sarai and other projects. William of Rubruck, a Franciscan friar who conducted a mission to the Great Khan in 1253, observed even in Mongolia a "young Russian ... [who] was skilled in making houses which is a profitable craft among them [the Mongols]."[7] As master craftsmen were removed, artisanal activity and its quality within the Rus lands declined.

Recovery was slow and uneven. Mongol exemptions of the Russian Church, its clergy, monks, and dependent peasants from tribute payments eased the economic burdens on a small portion of the population. New construction of masonry churches and other buildings, which required both relatively expensive materials and skilled labor, began to occur at the end of the thirteenth century. During the fourteenth century members of the Novgorodian elite acquired urban real estate and large tracts of land in the surrounding rural districts. Rents paid by peasants who lived in villages on the newly created landed estates contributed to family fortunes that distinguished and supported Novgorod's boyar ruling elite for generations. The boyars, along with archbishops and monastery abbots, contributed portions of their wealth for the construction of masonry fortifications as well as the small, limestone churches with a new trefoil roof design that would characterize Novgorodian churches for the next two centuries. Among the artists who decorated their interiors with icons and frescoes was Theophanes the Greek. Arriving in Novgorod from Constantinople in 1370, he contributed to a revitalization of the pictorial arts with his innovative composition, elongated figures, use of color, and brush techniques.

Vladimir, although nominally the main princely seat of northeastern Rus, never fully recovered from the blows inflicted by the Mongols. But other towns in northeastern Rus grew. One of these was Moscow, a relatively small outpost that had become the seat of a principality set aside by Alexander Nevsky for his youngest son. It nonetheless took the Vladimir-Suzdal region almost a quarter of a century longer than

The Church of the Transfiguration of Our Saviour on Ilyina street in Novgorod was built in 1374 and contains numerous frescoes by Theophanes the Greek. The decorative designs on the exterior walls and drum as well as the trefoil (triple-arched) roofline (later replaced but paralleled by the decorations) are among the features that distinguished the churches of Novgorod in the late fourteenth century. Alaexis/Creative Commons Attribution Share-Alike 2.5 Generic license.

Novgorod to display signs of economic improvement, and even then there were fewer masonry building projects there than in Novgorod. But, the construction of Moscow's kremlin in 1367–68 was conducted on a scale unknown elsewhere in northern Rus. To build the fort thousands of laborers hauled limestone and rubble over the ice of the Moscow River from a quarry more than thirty miles away.

Many factors tempered the rate of recovery in Rus. Mongol assaults tapered off in the 1320s but did not cease. Tribute drained wealth from the population, whose size and assets were already diminished. Inter-princely conflicts added to social stress and the depletion of resources. Famines occurred repeatedly throughout the fourteenth century. Even more disastrously, the Black Death reached the northern Rus lands in 1352. Chroniclers recorded grim images of the plague's impact in Pskov, a town located to the southwest of Novgorod: "A man would start to spit blood and the third day he would die; and the dead were everywhere. . . . The priests were unable even to bury the dead because in one night before matins they would bring twenty, even thirty, dead persons to the church." After the archbishop of Novgorod, responding to an appeal from the people of Pskov, visited the city and gave the people his blessing, "he went from them to Novgorod, and on the third day of the month of June he died." The plague spread through Novgorod and its hinterlands as well as throughout the Rus lands, south to Kiev, and east to Suzdal. Among the plague's victims were the grand prince, Semeon Ivanovich; two of his sons; and the metropolitan of the Orthodox Church. As the chronicler expressed it, "It was a terrifying, sudden and fast death, and there were fear and great trembling among all people."[8] The Black Death reappeared, along with fire and drought, just before Grand Prince Dmitrii Ivanovich undertook construction of the kremlin, making its completion even more difficult and remarkable. The Black Death, which reoccurred frequently until the 1420s, and other natural disasters continued to afflict the Rus lands approximately once every five years from the mid-fourteenth through the late fifteenth centuries.

Scholars disagree about the nature and degree of the economic, cultural, and even psychological impacts of the Mongol invasion and domination over the Rus. What is less controversial, however, is that under these difficult circumstances the Rus principalities underwent a political transformation. Kievan Rus fragmented. During the fourteenth century its western and southwestern principalities, including Kiev, slipped from Mongol control and were incorporated into Poland and Lithuania. Ryurikid princes and their Mongol overlords continued to rule the remaining northern Rus principalities: Suzdalia, which was subdivided into Vladimir, Rostov, Suzdal, Tver, and Moscow, among others; Novgorod to their west; and Ryazan. Of these, both the Mongols and the Church, albeit motivated by different interests, fostered the elevation of the Moscow branch of the dynasty. Its members, who became the grand princes of Vladimir, oversaw the creation of a new Russian state, Muscovy, which would eventually encompass all of northern Rus and overpower its Mongol masters.

The Mongol khans' support for Moscow's princes developed from their demands for tribute. Initially the khans stationed their own agents in the Rus lands to oversee its collection and delivery. But during the early decades of the fourteenth century the Mongols shifted those responsibilities to the Rus princes. When Khan Uzbek became disappointed with the way the reigning grand prince, Mikhail Yaroslavich, was performing those tasks, he broke his predecessors' custom of confirming the dynasty's most senior, eligible member as grand prince. Instead, the khan gave the grand princely throne to a prince from Moscow, Yurii Danilovich, who was ineligible for that position according to the dynasty's succession system. The khan also gave his sister in marriage to Yurii. Mikhail, however, resisted the transfer of power with armed force. During the battle he captured Yurii's wife, who died while in his custody. The khan placed Mikhail on trial in 1319. His accusers charged: "You ... fought with [the khan's envoy] and you killed many Tatars; and you collected the Khan's tribute for yourself and did not give it to the Khan ... and you poisoned the wife of Prince [Yurii]."[9] Mikhail was executed, but his sons continued to bid for the Vladimir throne. Their dubious techniques, including highway robbery and the murder of Yurii, resulted, however, only in the execution of one brother and a brief reign as grand prince for another. Finally, in 1327, Uzbek appointed Yurii's brother Ivan, who became known as Ivan I Kalita, grand prince. Thereafter, with a single, brief exception, Moscow princes consistently held the position and used it to shape a new realm of Muscovy and, eventually, to challenge the Tatar overlords who had elevated them to the highest position in the Rus lands.

The success of Yurii and his brother Ivan depended in part on their relationship to Novgorod and its commerce with Gotland, Lübeck, and other Baltic German towns. Under the terms of treaties concluded by the 1260s, Novgorodian merchants exported locally produced honey and wax as well as sable and other luxury fur pelts, collected from the Finnic tribes dwelling as far away as the Ob river. In exchange they received copper, tin, lead, iron, and other metal products; textiles and dyes; amber and glass; and beer and wine. Most importantly, they imported silver, which during the fourteenth century became the Mongols' preferred form of tribute payment.

Novgorod's leaders also concluded commercial treaties with Vladimir. European goods began to flow through Novgorod and Suzdalia to the markets of Sarai, where they joined the commercial traffic along the great Silk Road that stretched from China to Europe. Russian merchants returned from Sarai with glass and glazed pottery, silks, and other finery from Asia. In the yard surrounding the stone house that belonged to the descendants of the late thirteenth-century Novgorodian mayor (*posadnik*) Yurii Mishinich, archaeologists have unearthed sherds of the glazed pottery imported from the Golden Horde; these discoveries reflect both the range of the commercial network that stretched from Sarai to Novgorod and the wealth held by generations of the Novgorodian oligarchic families. Novgorod's commercial wealth, especially its silver imports, also became important for fulfilling tribute obligations to the khan. Novgorod's preference for Yurii of Moscow, who actively defended its leaders commercial interests, was a pivotal factor in his ability to win the khan's favor.

Assisted by their relationships with Novgorod as well as with the khans, the Moscow princes' control over the grand princely throne remained secure until the 1370s. At that time the Golden Horde was experiencing multiple problems. It too had suffered from the plague. The disintegration of other components of the Mongol Empire, moreover, was disrupting the Silk Road and causing the Golden Horde's commercial revenues to decline. These and other factors resulted in internal political discord, marked by a rapid turnover of rulers and the division of the Golden Horde among multiple, competing khans. Out of this turmoil a Mongol military commander, Mamai, achieved prominence. By 1378, however, he was confronting one of his fiercest rivals, Toqtamïsh, who emerged from the eastern portion of Juchi's ulus. Anxious to build up his forces against Toqtamïsh, Mamai pressed Grand Prince Dmitrii Ivanovich, grandson of Ivan I Kalita, for tribute.

Hindered by a drop in silver imports by Novgorod, Dmitrii did not immediately meet Mamai's demands. When the impatient Mongol commander gathered an army to force compliance, Dmitrii drew upon the enhanced military resources of his principality, enlarged by his forefathers, to assemble his own army. In September 1380, at the field of Kulikovo, near the Don River, "the two mighty hosts clashed in battle" and engaged, as the chronicler described it, in such "a fierce struggle and most evil slaughter [that] the blood ran like water and a numberless multitude of dead fell on both sides—on the Tatar and on the Russian." At one point in the battle, "the Tatars ... gain[ed] the upper hand and ... many illustrious great princes ... fell to the ground like trees. Grand Prince Dmitrii Ivanovich, himself, was unsaddled; and then, when he

Stylized figures of Russian warriors (left), led by Prince Dmitrii Donskoy, battle the Mongols (right), led by the military commander Mamai, at Kulikovo in 1380. Despite the Russian victory, the khans of the Golden Horde remained suzerains over the northern Rus principalities for another half century after the battle. Anonymous, seventeenth-century ms. "Skazanie o Mamaevom poboishche." From E. Mishina, Russkaya gravyura na dereve, XVII–XVIII vv. (St. Petersburg, n.d.).

mounted another horse, the Tatars again unhorsed him and wounded him. So, wearied, he was obliged to go from the battlefield."[10] But the Rus, employing a military tactic they had learned from the Tatars, had kept part of their army in reserve. When the fresh units joined the battle, Mamai and the exhausted remnants of his army fled.

The victory at Kulikovo did not end Mongol domination. Two years later, Toqtamïsh, having crushed Mamai, launched a campaign to reestablish Mongol authority over the rebellious Rus. This time, at the approach of the Tatar forces, Dmitrii abandoned Moscow. Breaching Moscow's fortifications, Toqtamïsh's forces "entered the city, ... and a great slaughter took place ... and the city was set aflame, and they plundered all the goods and the wealth and put people to the sword."[11] Despite Toqtamïsh's victory, Dmitrii came to regard the grand principality of Vladimir as his patrimony and left it in his will to his eldest son, Vasilii, without acknowledging the need for a patent from the khan. He furthermore dared to imagine a time when "a change regarding the Horde" might take place and his "children [would] not have to give Tatar tribute ... to the Horde." He left instructions that if such circumstances were to arise, "then the tribute ... that each of my sons collects in his patrimonial principality shall be his."[12]

The Golden Horde, indeed, remained intact for only another fifty years after the Battle of Kulikovo. Timur (Tamerlane) defeated his former client Toqtamïsh and destroyed the main urban and commercial centers of the Golden Horde from the Volga to the Black Sea, compromising its economic foundation. By the second quarter of the fifteenth century the political stability of the Golden Horde, centered at Sarai, had deteriorated and it was splintering into multiple hordes, occupying different sectors of the Golden Horde's realm: the Great Horde, which remained centered on the lower Volga and was later replaced by the Khanate of Astrakhan; the Crimean Khanate, which formed to its west; the Khanate of Kazan, centered on the mid-Volga; and the Nogai who nomadized the steppe. These new polities vied with one another as well as with Lithuania and with the northern Rus principalities, led by Moscow, for dominance over the region.

But the northern Rus principalities were not united. Dmitrii's predecessors had annexed some principalities, and their rulers, along with their retainers, had become subordinates of the Moscow prince. But others, most importantly Tver, Suzdal, Ryazan, and Novgorod, none of which had joined Dmitrii's coalition against Mamai, remained independent of Vladimir. At the death of Dmitrii's son, Vasilii I, in 1425, the grand principality of Vladimir was still only one of several in northern

Rus, and the rulers of the expanding state of Lithuania were extending their influence over them all. Tver and Ryazan both entertained close relations with Lithuania. Novgorod occasionally selected Lithuanian princes as alternatives to Moscow rulers. Even Vasilii I recognized the power of Lithuania, naming his father-in-law, the Lithuanian grand prince Vitovt, one of several guardians for his young son, Vasilii II.

After Vitovt died in 1430, Vasilii II became engaged in a bitter conflict with his uncle and cousins, who claimed his throne. During the struggle, which lasted a quarter of a century, Tatars then migrating toward the mid-Volga, where they would found the Khanate of Kazan, captured Vasilii. Following his release Vasilii was seized by his cousin, who blinded, deposed, and confined him again. Nonetheless, aided by loyal Moscow courtiers, Vasilii had by 1456 recovered his throne, eliminated his challengers, and vanquished their supporters. He formed an alliance with Tver and subdued Novgorod, which had favored his opponents. The central positions of Moscow among the lands of Rus and of Vasilii II as its prince were confirmed.

The Church also contributed to Moscow's primacy. Even as the Golden Horde khans singled out the Moscow princes, the Church fashioned an ideology that justified and legitimized the Moscow princes' growing power. In the decades immediately following the Mongol invasion, the metropolitans of the Church, who remained based in the ruins of Kiev, had attempted to minister to their entire Orthodox flock in all the Rus principalities. In 1299, however, Metropolitan Maksim transferred his residence from Kiev to northeastern Rus. While continuing to claim jurisdiction over the entire metropolitanate, his successor Metropolitan Petr favored Moscow, where he was buried in 1326 "in the church [of the Dormition of the Most Pure Theotokos] ... which he, himself, began to build together with his [spiritual] son, ... Ivan Danilovich [Ivan I Kalita], and where, with his own hands, he laid the foundation of his grave."[13] Petr's identification with Moscow persisted. His burial site quickly became a holy shrine. After being recognized by the Church as a saint in 1339, he was widely regarded as a special protector of Moscow.

Sergei of Radonezh (d. 1392), named a saint in the mid-fifteenth century, also became closely associated with Moscow and its princes. Unlike Metropolitan Petr, Sergei was a charismatic monk and a central figure in the monastic movement that gained momentum throughout the northern Rus lands from the middle of the fourteenth century. In contrast to the urban monasteries established in previous centuries, the new monasteries were located far from well-populated, disease-ridden towns.

They attracted monks who, possibly influenced by the controversial Byzantine hesychast movement that valued mystical experience and individual spiritual development, sought isolated locations where they could lead contemplative lives. Sergei of Radonezh located his hermitage in the 1330s at what is now Sergiev Posad (formerly Zagorsk) about forty-five miles northeast of Moscow. As a monastic community formed around him, he founded the Holy Trinity Monastery in 1354. Over the next century Sergei's disciples and their followers established other monasteries, contributing to the creation of a network of more than 150 monasteries, including the St. Cyril-Beloozero about 375 miles north of Moscow and the Solovetsky on the White Sea. Supported by donations in land and other forms of wealth, the monasteries built cathedrals and fortifications and served as spiritual centers across the Russian north.

Sergei's asceticism and high moral standards were spiritually inspirational. But by officiating at the christening ceremonies of two of Prince Dmitrii's sons and being in attendance at Dmitrii's funeral, he also demonstrated his close ties to the Moscow princes. One of his hagiographers, moreover, asserted that on the eve of the Battle of Kulikovo, Sergei had blessed Dmitrii and his army and his prayers had been instrumental in eliciting divine assistance that secured their victory. Donations made by Vasilii I and his brother Yurii, among others, made the Holy Trinity Monastery, in contrast to its humble beginnings, one of the largest landowners in the Russian lands. Monks associated with it also contributed to the enhancement of Moscow. The icon and fresco painter Andrei Rublev (c. 1370–1430), who spent the early years of his career at the Trinity monastery and later painted the icon "Old Testament Trinity" for it, assisted Theophanes the Greek, who had been commissioned by Vasilii I to paint the iconostasis for the Cathedral of the Annunciation in the kremlin.

The Church, however, faced its own dilemmas. After the metropolitan died in 1431, there was no one at the helm of the Russian Church for six critical years, during which domestic warfare raged, making communication and transportation dangerous. Finally in 1437, Isidor arrived from Constantinople to be the new metropolitan. His focus, however, was to draw the Russian Church into a union between Orthodoxy and the Roman Church, a prerequisite for securing European aid against the Ottoman Turks then threatening Byzantium with annihilation. Within six months of his arrival, Isidor left again, leading a Russian delegation to the Council of Ferrara-Florence, which in 1439 united the eastern and western churches, formally divided since

1054. But the Russian Church had entertained hostile attitudes toward the Latin Church since at least the destruction of Constantinople during the Fourth Crusade (1204). Consequently, when Isidor returned to Moscow from Italy as a cardinal and papal legate, Vasilii II and the Rus clerics rejected the union, which required recognition of papal supremacy and infallibility as well as some Latin definitions of dogma. They deposed Isidor and imprisoned him, leaving the Church without a head while the dynastic wars engulfed the Russian lands.

Resolution of the church crisis, when it came, became intertwined with the Church's elevation of the Moscow princes. In the absence of a metropolitan, others in the ecclesiastic community, notably the bishop of Ryazan, Iona, and the abbot of the St. Cyril-Beloozero, had assisted Vasilii II during his fight for the grand princely throne. Almost immediately after he regained it, Vasilii II broke the tradition of requesting a new metropolitan from Constantinople, considered by the Russian clerics to have fallen into apostasy for its union with Rome. Instead, he supported the Russian bishops' selection of Iona to lead the Russian Church. After Constantinople fell to the Turks in 1453, interpreted as divine confirmation of the Russian Church's position, Iona and other leading ecclesiastical figures promoted the notion that Moscow had become the center of the true Orthodox Church, heir to Kiev, its original Rus center. They claimed that saints, such as the former metropolitan Petr and the monk Sergei of Radonezh, extended their protection particularly over Moscow. They also interpreted Vasilii's rejection of Isidor and the church union as the fulfillment of his divinely appointed duty as grand prince of Moscow to defend Orthodoxy. The new self-justifying church ideology also elevated the grand prince of Moscow above his peers and recognized Moscow as the center of the lands of Rus.

The Mongol invasion had crushed Kievan Rus. As its western principalities were absorbed into Poland and the newly formed Lithuania, its northern components remained under the rule of Ryurikid princes and their Mongol overlords. The Mongols, however, selected the disqualified line of princes from Moscow to hold the senior position of grand prince of Vladimir. Using their connections with the commercial center of Novgorod, the princes of Moscow met the Mongols' demands for tribute but also annexed territories and subordinated neighboring principalities to become the strongest among the northern Rus principalities and retain their dominance even when the Golden Horde disintegrated. The victory of Vasilii II in his inter-princely war and the ideological support he received from the Church converged to create a legacy for his son and heir. When Ivan III succeeded his father in 1462, he was the most powerful among the Russian princes. He and his successors would use their positions to add the remaining Rus principalities to their own to form the state of Muscovy and successfully confront their neighbors, the Tatar khanates and Lithuania.

CHAPTER 3

Muscovy

The Late Ryurikids and Early Romanovs (1462–1689)

In 1472, Sophia (Zoë) Palaeologa, the niece of the last Byzantine emperor, became the second wife of Ivan III, a widower. Her arrival from Rome ushered into Moscow a wave of European influence. With her encouragement, Ivan and, later, their son Vasilii III invited Pietro Antonio Solari, also known as Pietro Fryazin, as well as Marco Ruffo, Aristotele Fioravanti, and other Italian Renaissance artists, architects, and engineers to their realm. Their expertise contributed to the construction of the ensemble of masonry palaces and cathedrals in the Moscow kremlin that remains the signature symbol of Russia. The gold cupolas of the Orthodox cathedrals rising above the red brick walls, gates, and towers of the triangular fortress became an emblem, representing both the long-standing spiritual foundation of the Rus principalities and also the material power of the grand prince who bore the responsibility to preserve and defend them. But the balance and proportion of these edifices, characteristic of the Italian Renaissance, as well as their new façades and decorative motifs also represented Russia's willingness to absorb and adapt selected European engineering techniques and cultural styles. Just like the Scandinavian, Byzantine, and Mongol influences on the Rus principalities in previous centuries, elements of European culture would affect Russia's future development.

The renovations of the kremlin constituted only one of the policies inaugurated by Ivan III that would alter the appearance and character of his realm. When he took the throne in 1462, he faced no domestic opposition. While still securing his own ruling position, his father Vasilii II had named the nine-year-old Ivan his co-ruler; arranged the boy's marriage to his first wife, the daughter of the prince of Tver;

The Cathedral of St. Michael the Archangel (left), constructed by the architect Alevisio Novi (1505–09); the Annunciation cathedral (center), built by masters from Pskov (1484–89); and the Dormition (Assumption) Cathedral (right), restored by Aristotele Fioravanti of Bologna (completed 1479), were constructed under the sponsorship of Grand Prince Ivan III and his son Vasilii III. Among the oldest edifaces in the complex that distinguishes the Moscow kremlin, they represent a blend of Russian and European architectural influences that are embodied in the ensemble. ©Vladimir Wrangel/Shutterstock, NY/1021005.

and in his will bequeathed to his "oldest son, Ivan, ... [his] patrimony, the Grand Princedom" without obtaining a patent from the Mongol khan to legitimize the succession.[1] But as the fragmentation of the Golden Horde gave way to competition among the new Tatar khanates, Lithuania, and the northern Rus principalities, new challenges emerged. Over the next century Ivan III, his son Vasilii III, and grandson Ivan IV, confronting their rivals, expanded their realm to both the east and the west. In the process they unified the northern Rus principalities and created a centralized monarchy known as Muscovy.

Ivan's initial concerns were to strengthen his own realm and its position in the region. Convinced that Novgorod was planning to transfer its political and ecclesiastical allegiance to Lithuania, Ivan forcibly annexed it in 1478, arrested its leaders, and exiled them to Moscow. Seven years later he subjugated Tver. The result was a series of wars with Lithuania, which ended in 1522 with Muscovy acquiring Lithuanian borderlands, including the old Rus centers, Smolensk and Chernigov. During the same period Ivan and his heirs confronted the Tatars. In 1480, Muscovite and Great Horde forces shot arrows at each other from opposite banks of the Ugra River. This encounter, known as the Stand on the Ugra, has traditionally been interpreted as the end of the "Tatar yoke" or Mongol domination over the Rus principalities. Muscovy and the emergent Tatar khanates nonetheless engaged in a prolonged power struggle that resulted in Muscovy's annexation of the Khanates of Kazan and Astrakhan in 1552 and 1556, respectively.

These victories radically changed the demographic composition of Muscovy. From Kazan alone it acquired populations of not only Muslim Tatars but also Turkic-speaking Chuvash as well as Finnic-speaking Udmurts (Votiaks), Mari (Cheremis), and Mordvinians; most of them were hunters, beekeepers, fishermen, and farmers, and observed animist religions. Turkic-speaking nomads, including some Nogai, descendants of peoples of the Golden Horde, and Bashkirs, who dwelled between the Volga River and the Ural Mountains, also recognized the Muscovite ruler. In the immediate aftermath of the conquest, characterized by Orthodox churchmen as a victory of Christianity over Islam, Muscovite officials evicted Kazan's Tatar residents, resettling them outside the reconstructed city walls, and transformed the city into an Orthodox center inhabited by Russian officials, an archbishop and other clergy, soldiers, and merchants. Later, however, Muscovite administrators adopted a more tolerant approach. They secured the annexed territories, in part by co-opting local leaders into their own social and political hierarchy. They collected tribute from the commoners but refrained from forcing the non-Orthodox peoples to convert to Christianity and only gradually and indirectly, through colonization, interfered with their traditional lifestyles.

To govern, defend, and continue to expand their realm, the Moscow grand princes centralized the military and administrative functions of all the Rus principalities they had subjugated under their control. Shortly after his conquest of Novgorod, Ivan III introduced military reforms that created an army subject directly to the grand prince's command and particularly well suited to fight other Russian forces and Tatar steppe warriors. It consisted of cavalrymen, who, in lieu of salaries, received landed service estates (*pomest'ia*), initially carved out of lands confiscated from the Novgorodian elite, and rents paid by their resident peasants. The skillful way the cavalrymen held "the bridle, the bow, the short sword, the javelin, and the whip, in their hands all at the same time" greatly impressed Sigismund von Herberstein, the Hapsburg ambassador to the court of Vasilii III.[2] After the conquests of the Volga khanates, loyal Tatars, similarly skilled as mounted archers, augmented the Russian servicemen, who were by this time based throughout Muscovy. To fight western foes as well as to conquer and defend fortified towns, Ivan III and his successors supplemented the cavalry with units trained to use artillery and other firearms—weapons being developed in European countries. Aristotele Fioravanti not only oversaw the reconstruction of the Dormition Cathedral in the Moscow kremlin, but also taught the Muscovites methods of bronze casting, an improvement over traditional iron casting. Ivan III founded the first cannon and gunpowder factories in Moscow. Production and import of firearms enabled his grandson Ivan IV to add a unit of musketeers (*streltsy*) to his army in 1550, shortly before his chief western adversaries, Lithuania and Poland, created similar, but smaller corps. The numbers of these salaried foot soldiers, who were based in towns and on the frontier, rose from 3,000 to 20,000–25,000 by the end of the century. The *pomest'e*-based cavalry nonetheless formed the core of Muscovy's army into the seventeenth century.

To command the army and manage the widening range of state business, the grand princes drew upon their boyars, their highest-ranking courtiers. They also oversaw the development of a central administrative apparatus to carry out their policies. Evolving from a few literate elite slaves, sons of priests, merchants, and foreigners, who served Ivan III, it became a complex set of specialized chancelleries during the reign of Ivan IV. The grand princely government introduced and implemented new law codes, appointed governors and other provincial officials, and imposed central Muscovite authority throughout its expanding domain. It also conducted diplomatic activity with other countries. With the expansion of state responsibilities the stature of the grand prince rose. Although some scholars have concluded the monarch's seemingly autocratic power was actually tempered by the customary and practical need for consensual governance, all participants in formulating and implementing government policies avowed that the grand prince was the sole source of the authority they exercised.

Russian Church officials justified the placement of the grand princes above all others in the dynasty, court, and country. From their theological perspective Moscow had become the center of Orthodoxy after Constantinople had formed the church union with Rome and then fallen to the Turks in 1453. Church leaders, correspondingly, considered Moscow's grand princes as divinely charged to protect the Orthodox Church and Muscovy, its terrestrial base, and referred to them in increasingly elevated terms. Metropolitan Zosima identified Ivan III as the heir of Constantine, the first Christian emperor of Byzantium, and of the divinely inspired St. Vladimir, who had converted the Rus to Orthodoxy. During the reign of Vasilii III, Joseph, the influential abbot of the Volokolamsk monastery, proclaimed that "by nature the king is like unto all men, but in authority he is like unto God Almighty."[3] In 1547, when Ivan IV reached his majority at the age of sixteen, Metropolitan Makarii, officiating at a grand ceremony held in the Dormition Cathedral, crowned him not only grand prince but also tsar, implicitly claiming for him and his heirs a status equivalent to emperors and khans for whom the title had previously been reserved.

The supreme power of Muscovy's rulers impressed foreign visitors. To Sigismund von Herberstein it appeared that all Muscovites considered that "the will of the prince is the will of God and that whatever the prince does, he does by the will of God."[4] This power intimidated their subjects. When villagers on the White Sea coast found the Englishman Richard Chancellor, who had accidentally discovered Muscovy while searching for a northern sea route to Asia in 1553, they offered food and shelter to him and his shipmates. But fearing the consequences of acting without the tsar's permission, they refused to trade with the Englishmen "without the knowledge and consent of the king [tsar]" and sent to distant Moscow for instructions.[5] Members of Muscovite society also regarded the tsar as a personal protector, a dispenser of justice and mercy. Orina, the widow of the *pomeshchik*-cavalryman Oleksandr Ushakov, turned to the tsar rather than her family or the Church when she was "evict[ed] from her home" by her sons, who refused to support her. Responding to her petition, tsarist officials set aside a portion of her late husband's estate for her maintenance "until she entered a convent or died."[6]

Muscovy's expansion and the might of its rulers rested on a growing population and economy. Widespread adoption of the more productive three-field rotation system enabled many peasants to pay rents to military servicemen as well as higher taxes to the government. Richard Chancellor, traveling through the countryside, observed that "their fields yield such store of corn [grain] that in conveying it towards Moscow sometimes in a forenoon a man shall see seven hundred or eight hundred sleds, going and coming, laden with corn and salt fish."[7] Commercial activity also expanded. Chancellor secured rights for English merchants to trade with Muscovy; within two decades the Dutch were also using the northern route discovered by Chancellor and the port of Arkhangelsk, built in the early 1580s. Arriving just as the commercial fair opened in June, the English and Dutch purchased shipbuilding materials, cordage, and flax and, like the Poles and German merchants who had long used overland and Baltic routes to reach Muscovy, furs, hides, and wax. They departed before the fair closed on September 1 so they could sail around Norway before stormy seas prevented their passage. Muscovite merchants then hastened to transport the textiles, metals, silver coins, and other imported goods southward. Farther south, Muscovite control over the Volga River and its markets opened direct trade with western Siberia, Central Asia, Persia, and the nomadic Nogai, which yielded silks, cotton, and horses among other goods. Taxes on agricultural land, customs fees, and tribute from the non-Orthodox populations brought increased revenues that supported the enlarged government and army.

Ivan IV "the Terrible," however, launched policies that reversed the political, military, and economic gains achieved by his predecessors. Attempting to understand this enigmatic figure and his policies, scholars have depicted him in ways that range from a ruthless ruler intent upon eliminating all limits on monarchical power to a person suffering either from mental illness or mercury poisoning caused by medication administered for a painful skeletal disease. Whatever his personal characteristics, the political system he inherited and the theories that legitimized it offered no mechanism for tempering the excesses of a ruler who declined the counsel of church hierarchs, boyars, administrative officials, and other traditional advisors.

Ivan IV initially continued his predecessors' policies. His decision to invade Livonia (modern Estonia and Latvia), however, provoked both Sweden and Lithuania to declare war on Muscovy. Under the pressure of prolonged war and its mounting costs, Muscovy's century-long string of successes snapped. In the midst of the Livonian War Ivan, accusing his boyars and the metropolitan of treachery, threatened to abdicate. He subsequently agreed to remain on the throne but also created a separate royal domain, known as the *oprichnina*, to which he attached large portions of Muscovy and favored members of the court and merchant elites. Before the *oprichnina* was disbanded in 1572, thousands of its special guardsmen (*oprichniki*), dressed in black robes and riding black horses, terrorized the country. They confiscated estates of mighty and minor landowners, exiling some, torturing and executing others; sacked the city of Novgorod; and drove one metropolitan from office and then deposed and murdered his successor. Taking advantage of the debilitating turmoil, the Crimean Tatars, still unreconciled to Muscovy's annexation of the Volga khanates, breached Muscovy's defenses and set fire to Moscow in 1571. In separate offensives begun in the late 1570s, the Polish-Lithuanian Commonwealth (formed in 1569) and Sweden besieged Pskov and threatened Novgorod, forcing Ivan IV to accept defeat. In 1582–83, he ceded to them his acquisitions in Livonia and Lithuania, his territories north and west of Novgorod, and with the exception of the mouth of the Neva River, all Muscovy's coastal territories on the Gulf of Finland.

Ivan's policies were also economically catastrophic. Assessments for military construction, musketeers, gunpowder, ransoming prisoners of war, and other military-related expenses tripled peasants' taxes, prompting many in northwestern and central Muscovy to abandon their villages. By the early 1580s, the peasant population of the Novgorod region, reduced to about 20 percent of its size at the beginning of the century, cultivated barely 6 percent of the fields. Among the deserted villages and fallow fields, small numbers survived on the sites of their homes, burned by the Poles or the Swedes. Around Moscow only 13 percent to 14 percent of arable land remained under cultivation. Depopulation lowered government revenues; it also reduced the rental incomes of the cavalrymen, some of whom, unable to arm themselves for combat, avoided mobilization or deserted.

The options for the impoverished were few. Some, in accordance with a long-standing Muscovite practice known as debt servitude or limited service contract slavery, borrowed money and agreed to work for their creditors for a year to pay the interest on their loans. When they failed to repay the principal at the end of the loan period, they became slaves of their creditors, serving on their behalf in the army, tending their fields, or working in their households. Slaves made up 5 percent to 15 percent of Muscovy's population but reached the upper level of that range in the late sixteenth and early seventeenth centuries.

Another option was flight—to estates of large landowners and monasteries, which offered subsidies and protection; to towns; and to the new southern and eastern frontiers, which, in contrast to the economically depressed conditions in the heartland of Muscovy, offered fresh opportunities. In the south, fugitives found employment on defense lines that from the 1570s were being constructed to impede attacks by the Crimean Tatars and other nomads. Runaways worked as carpenters, blacksmiths, or common laborers, building palisades, earthworks, and man-made barriers on the lines or joining garrisons as soldiers. Some, taking advantage of the relative security they provided, settled behind the fortified lines. Others ventured beyond the ever advancing southern frontier to join the Cossacks whose communities or "hosts," led by elected atamans, consisted of a diverse mix of individuals from Poland, the Tatar khanates, and the northern Caucasus as well as Muscovy. Naming their hosts for the rivers, such as the Dnieper, Don, and the Yaik, along which they settled, and operating beyond the reach of all the surrounding states, the Cossacks—sometime pirates and bandits, sometime hired border guards, and sometime auxiliary units in regular armies—offered sanctuary to the disaffected: slaves, adventurers, escaped captives and convicts, and also runaway peasants and soldiers.

Refugees from the interior also fled eastward, beyond Kazan, where the entrepreneurial Stroganov family was developing millions of acres of forested lands, granted by Ivan IV. Wealthy merchants who had made fortunes in salt production and fur trading in the northern territories east of the Dvina River, the Stroganovs brought thousands of colonists to operate their new saltworks and other enterprises. But the influx of Russians destroyed the hunting and fishing grounds of the indigenous populations who, as the Stroganovs reported to the tsar, attacked the settlers, drove off horses and cattle, "burned settlements and hamlets, grain and hay, took peasants, their wives, and children captive," and also "burned the salt works and mills."[8]

Among those hired by the Stroganovs to defend their enterprises was Yermak Timofeevich, a Don Cossack who had served in the Livonian War. While pursuing some of the attackers, Yermak led a band of 840 Cossacks and settlers across the Ural Mountains, defeated the Tatar khan of Sibir in 1582, and claimed western Siberia for the tsar. Yermak's actions opened the way for the conquest of Siberia. In 1632, Petr Beketov, a *streltsy* officer, with a unit of thirty Cossacks, subjugated the Yakut people and built a fort overlooking the mid-Lena river, where the town of Yakutsk quickly developed. Another detachment, led by Ivan Moskvitin, reached the Sea of Okhotsk in 1639. His men made their way back to Yakutsk two years later, bearing a fortune in sable and black fox pelts. In 1647, another band of Cossacks returned to the region Moskvitin had explored. Using their firearms, they defeated the hostile, local Tungus populace and founded Okhotsk, Russia's first foothold on the Pacific Ocean. Similar groups reached Kamchatka by the end of the seventeenth century. The Treaty of Nerchinsk, concluded with China in 1689, set the southern boundary of Muscovite-controlled Siberia in the mountains north of the Amur River. The Cossack explorers and adventurers were followed by administrators, soldiers, clerics, tribute collectors, fur traders, settlers, and exiled prisoners. They

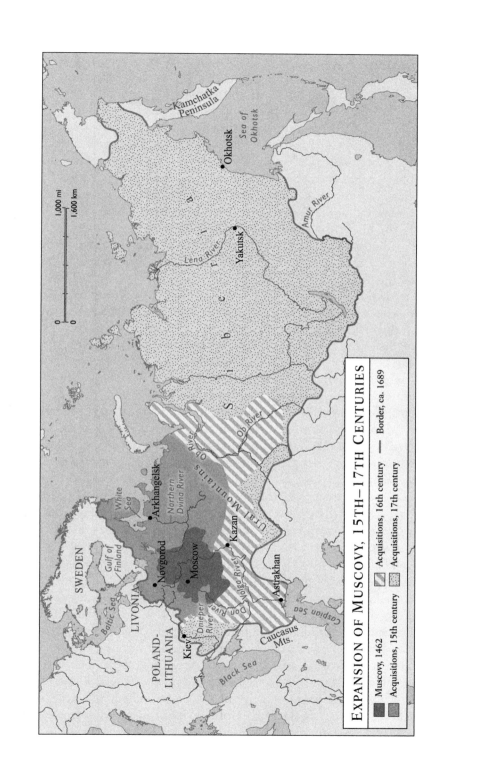

EXPANSION OF MUSCOVY, 15TH–17TH CENTURIES

Muscovy, 1462

Acquisitions, 15th century

Acquisitions, 16th century

Acquisitions, 17th century

Border, ca. 1689

quickly overwhelmed the indigenous populations—estimated at fewer than 200,000 persons, divided into more than 100 different tribes, and scattered over more than five million square miles—and compelled them to pay tribute to the tsar, mainly in valuable luxury fur pelts.

The social disruption and economic damage resulting from Ivan IV's adventures persisted in the core of Muscovy well after the tsar's death in 1584. A political crisis compounded the ill effects of his legacy after his feeble-minded son and successor Feodor died in 1598 without leaving an heir. For the next fifteen years Muscovy endured a rapid succession of rulers, including Boris Godunov who had managed government affairs for his brother-in-law Feodor. Even before Godunov's death in 1605, champions of competing boyar clans were vying for power with each other as well as with pretenders claiming to be Dmitrii, the youngest son of Ivan IV, who had reportedly died in 1591. The country descended into civil war. The Swedes, initially invited to assist one faction, seized Novgorod; their rivals, the Poles, occupied Moscow. Faced with the dismemberment of Muscovy and reacting to the prospect that the Polish king, a Catholic, might take the Muscovite throne, the leader of the Orthodox Church, whose position had been elevated from metropolitan to patriarch in 1589, took the initiative. While being held in confinement and starving, Patriarch Hermogen smuggled out letters calling for resistance. In response, first one and then a second national militia formed. Commanded by Prince Dmitrii Pozharsky and supported with funds raised by a butcher, Kozma Minin, the militias consisted of townsmen, provincial servicemen, troops from the pretenders' armies, and Don Cossacks. Although internally divided, this national liberal movement besieged the Polish garrison, which had retreated to the kremlin after burning the surrounding city of Moscow, and forced it to surrender in October 1612. The Time of Troubles, as this period is known, ended in 1613, when an assembly of the land elected a new tsar. Their choice was Michael Romanov, the sixteen-year-old, poorly educated cousin of Feodor, the last Ryurikid ruler.

Michael's ascension to the throne restored the previous order. The boyar duma, consisting of boyars as well as other high-ranking courtiers and administrative officials, regained leadership of a reconstituted court. The central chancelleries and appointed governors reestablished control over towns, local officials, and provincial military servicemen. The Orthodox Church reaffirmed its ecclesiastic dominance. Dynastic security remained elusive, however, until Michael produced an heir in 1629 and the Polish king gave up his claim to the Muscovite throne in 1634. Even then the perpetuation of the

A statue of Kozma Minin and Prince Dmitrii Pozharsky memorializes the two leaders of the national liberation movement that forced the surrender of a Polish garrison, leading to the end of the Time of Troubles. The monument is located in Red Square, just outside of the Moscow kremlin, where the Polish forces had been under siege for eighteen months. Steven Pavlov/Creative Commons Share-Alike 3.0 Unported license.

Romanov dynasty was not assured. Although Maria Miloslavskaya, the wife of Michael's son Alexis, gave birth to thirteen children, her death in 1669 and that of their eldest son in 1670 left the dynasty's fate dependent on the frail health of their two remaining sons and influenced Alexis's decision to remarry. His bride Natalia Naryshkina gave birth to a healthy son, the future Peter the Great, easing fears for the dynasty's future.

Reestablishment of political order encouraged economic recovery. Adam Olearius, a member of an embassy from Holstein in the 1630s, not only saw butchers, bakers, "the cattle market, and taverns selling beer, mead, and vodka," and an icon market in Moscow, but he also visited a bustling marketplace where "sellers of silk and cloth, goldsmiths, saddle-makers, shoemakers, tailors, furriers, belt- or girdle-makers ... , [and] hat makers" conducted their businesses; additionally, he observed "a casting works where many metal guns and large bells ... [were] made."[9] Improved domestic conditions also enabled Tsar Alexis to conduct the successful Thirteen Years' War against Poland-Lithuania (1654–67) and regain territories, including Smolensk and Chernigov, lost during the Time of Troubles. He also acquired the east bank of the Dnieper River and Kiev.

European technology and expertise contributed significantly to Muscovy's economic growth and military success. The Dutch, by the 1620s and 1630s, were heavily engaged in the iron industry, held monopolies on pitch and potash production, and were building a fleet for the Caspian Sea. European engineers were engaged in mining and in processing metals; European artisans manufactured silks and velvets, wine, glass, and paper; and European translators, physicians, and other professionals were employed at court and by the Muscovite elite. Before launching the Thirteen Years' War, moreover, Alexis adopted military reforms based on European technologies and tactics. He organized new formation infantry and dragoon regiments, which consisted of salaried, semi-regular infantrymen, who, equipped with firearms and trained and commanded by European officers, served for life. The new infantry, like the old cavalry, sustained huge losses during the war. But reinforced by repeated levies that conscripted tens of thousands of peasants, it was responsible for Muscovy's victory.

The military reforms, even before their full implementation during the war, had profound social repercussions, especially for the provincial cavalrymen, the mainstay of the old army, and for the peasantry. One effect was to reduce the value of the mounted archers, who had disdained the new infantry with its fire-arms and foreign officers. But rather than take away the landed estates they received for their service, a new law code, adopted in 1649, treated those estates as virtually hereditary. The code also affected their peasants. An earlier law code (1497) had permitted peasants to move "from village to village, [only] once a year for a week before and a week after St. George's Day in the autumn

[November 26]."[10] During the last years of his reign, Ivan IV, contending with mass peasant flight, had further restricted peasant mobility by closing the St. George's Day window in designated or "forbidden" years. The 1649 code not only recognized every year as "forbidden," making it illegal for peasants to leave their villages, but required the "return [of] fugitive peasants ... from flight ... to people of all ranks, without any statute of limitations." All peasants who fled from "hereditary estate owners and service landholders" to live on other estates or "as townsmen ..., or as musketeers, or as Cossacks, or as gunners, or as any other type of servicemen in ... the frontier towns" were henceforth to be returned to their villages.[11] While some of the old-style cavalrymen became impoverished and lost their status, others, their privileged access to land and peasant labor secured by the law code, gradually became landed gentry. Their peasants, in contrast, having no legal opportunity to move and subject to forcible return at any time, if discovered as fugitives, were transformed into serfs.

By the second half of the seventeenth century a wider range of European influences was penetrating Muscovy, stimulating extreme social reactions. Some members of the political elite, both in Moscow and the provinces, embraced elements of European secular culture. Tsar Alexis assembled such individuals in Moscow where they became fixtures at court and in government administration. Afanasii L. Ordin-Nashchokin, a native of Pskov, having negotiated the conclusion of the Thirteen Years' War, became chief of the Ambassadorial Chancellery and a boyar. His library collection, which contained works in Latin and other foreign languages, reflected his admiration for Europe. His successor in the Ambassadorial Chancellery, Artamon Sergeevich Matveev, rose from provincial service ranks to become a commander of a *streltsy* regiment. He married a Scottish woman and filled their home with European-style furnishings and decorations, including clocks and paintings. His wife, in contrast to elite Muscovite women who typically remained secluded from male company and out of public view, conversed with men and joined in the entertainments Matveev hosted. After arranging the tsar's marriage in 1671 to Natalia Naryshkina, Matveev was promoted to the rank of boyar. Like Ordin-Nashchokin, he helped make European styles fashionable among the social elite.

Alexis also developed an enthusiasm for Western cultural styles and science. While in Poland during the Thirteen Years' War, he admired the baroque architecture so much that, according to the physician Samuel Collins, he began "to model his Court and Edifices more stately, to furnish his Rooms with Tapestry, and contrive houses of pleasure abroad."[12] He possessed a German carriage, requested a telescope from the Danish ambassador, and at his wooden summer palace, constructed in the 1660s outside Moscow at Kolomenskoe, he had a ceiling decorated with a heliocentric design and signs of the zodiac. At Preobrazhenskoe, another royal estate, and also at a court theater organized by Matveev in Moscow, Alexis sponsored private European-style theatrical productions, performed by German and other foreign actors and accompanied by music and dancing. In 1667, moreover, the tsar engaged the Kiev-educated scholar, poet, and monk Semeon Polotsky to teach Latin, Polish, theology, and literature to his sons, Alexis (d.1670) and Feodor and also his daughter Sophia. Alexis did not, however, abandon traditional Russian culture. On the walls of the Kolomenskoe palace he hung portraits of Julius Caesar and Alexander the Great, but also filled its rooms with traditional Orthodox icons. He employed Samuel Collins as court physician, but when his son Alexis was dying, he sent an official to the home of a recently deceased sorceress to search for "roots, herbs, stones, and written spells which she used to help guard sick people from bewitchments" and to discover "whether she had taught her skills to anyone else" who might cure his son.[13]

Sophia—who served as regent (1682–89) for Feodor's heirs, her brother Ivan V and half-brother Peter I, and was the first woman to lead Muscovy since the mother of Ivan IV—also adopted Western social manners at court. Initially she adhered to the custom of remaining in seclusion, concealing herself when the young co-tsars formally received foreign diplomats or performed other public ceremonial duties. But she soon abandoned it. In 1684, when receiving a Swedish envoy, "the sovereign lady" appeared in person, "attended by ladies-in-waiting … and by several courtiers and at the sides [of the chamber] there also stood Prince Vasilii Vasil'evich Golitsyn and Ivan Mikhailovich Miloslavsky."[14] Golitsyn (1643–1714), Sophia's chief advisor and favorite, also admired Western styles. Among his eighteen carriages, the most valuable one, gilded, carved, and upholstered in black leather and red velvet, came from northern Europe.

But others spurned European cultural influences. One of the most vociferous among them was Patriarch Nikon, who ordered non-Orthodox Europeans living in Moscow to move to a suburb, called the German quarter, to protect Russians from what he considered the foreigners' impiety. He also condemned Western styles of painting that were being adopted for portraits of secular figures as well as religious icons, which he disfigured and smashed. The archpriest Avvakum agreed with him that "unseemly foreign painting has spread over our Russian land." Although he would leave an account of his experiences, reminiscent in form to European autobiographies, Avvakum was incensed by a Western-style image of "Our Saviour Emmanuel with a puffy face, and red lips, curly hair, fat arms and muscles, and stout legs and thighs."[15]

Both Nikon and Avvakum were members of a group of reformers, supported by Tsar Alexis, that sought to retain the purity of Russian Orthodoxy, especially at the parish level. But they became bitter opponents when Nikon decided to print new editions of service books and other religious texts, based on Greek rather than Russian manuscripts. This decision, coupled with his orders to change the manner of signing the cross, the wording of prayers, and other basic rituals and visual symbols, aroused intense opposition. Avvakum and a wide range of like-minded Muscovites, including boyars and commoners, laymen and clergy, men and women, regarded the Greek copies as corruptions of the true Orthodox texts and the other reforms as heretical deviations from ancient church custom. Interpreting an outbreak of plague as divine punishment for the adoption of Nikon's reforms, Avvakum and the Old Believers, as they became known, refused to accept his changes.

Nikon also lost the favor of the tsar. Despite his charges that it was Alexis who had been guilty of unlawfully "lord[ing] it over the Church ... enrich[ing] himself with sacred property ... [and compelling] the metropolitans, archbishops, bishops, priests, and all the ... clergy [to] serve him as slaves,"[16] a church council, held in 1666–67 and attended by the patriarchs of Alexandria and Antioch, deposed Nikon. It also excommunicated the schismatics, who were subsequently subjected to imprisonment, exile, and even execution. Avvakum was burned at the stake in 1681. The church schism, however, proved permanent. Despite their persecution, the Old Believers clung to their faith, challenging the spiritual authority of the official church and undermining its unity.

The uprisings and state violence associated with the church schism were only one expression of social tensions that mounted during the second half of the seventeenth century. An enlarged and increasingly impersonal central administration not only enforced unpopular laws, such as those against gambling, using and selling tobacco, and brewing alcoholic beverages, but also appeared to block access to the tsar by his subjects. Prevented from presenting a petition complaining about unfair taxes to Alexis in 1648, townsmen rioted. Supported by sympathetic armed *streltsy*, they murdered corrupt officials, looted the homes of the wealthy and powerful, and burned half of Moscow. In 1662, urban riots broke out again, this time in response to attempts to raise revenue for the war and its costly military reforms by substituting copper for silver coins, while Bashkirs and other non-Russian peoples staged uprisings protesting demands for higher tribute and the encroachment on their pastures by Russian peasants and Muslim refugees from the mid-Volga. In 1670–71, all of southeastern Muscovy erupted in the Stenka Razin rebellion. Razin, the leader of a band of Don Cossacks, seized the fortress at Astrakhan where the populace fatally threw their governor from a tower. Issuing a call to all those who wanted "to serve God and the Sovereign and the great Host ... [and] eliminate the traitors and the bloodsuckers of the peasant communities,"[17] he proceeded up the Volga, encouraging townsmen to turn on local officials, inciting serfs to murder their masters, and sparking renewed insurrections among the non-Russian Volga populations. Government forces finally captured, tortured, and brutally executed Razin. Then, sweeping through the rebellious regions, they executed thousands more, leaving gallows and beheaded and impaled bodies in their wake.

The victorious conclusion of the Thirteen Years' War, the removal of Patriarch Nikon, and the suppression of the rebellion demonstrated the power wielded by the Romanov tsar toward the end of the seventeenth century. An enlarged boyar duma, multiple chancelleries, and appointed provincial governors implemented his policies over a domain covering 5,600,000 square miles stretching from the Dnieper River to the Pacific Ocean. But tensions between opposing court factions, the Westernizing reformers and conservative traditionalists, the official church and schismatics, Russians and non-Russians, and between the limitations of a serf-based agricultural economy and the costs of engaging with Europe posed challenges for the Romanovs as they led Muscovy into the eighteenth century.

CHAPTER 4

The Petrine Revolution
(1689–1725)

In portraits, Tsar Peter the Great looks nothing like his father, Tsar Alexis Mikhailovich. The father wears a beard, the traditional Orthodox emblem of godliness; the son is clean-shaven. Like other men of his time, the father wears a caftan; the son is suited in armor. The symbols of the father's rule are Christian: on his chest rests a great cross, in his left hand, a cross-topped orb. The setting itself is icon-like. No Christian imagery appears in portraits of the son; here, Peter holds a telescope in his right hand, while to his left we see two sailing ships, emblematic of the practical, technological, and military focus of Peter's reign and its new goal of worldly glory. Even the names of the rulers differ: Tsar Alexis Mikhailovich bears a patronymic, derived from his father's name Michael and signifying Tsar Alexis's status as his father's heir and successor. Tsar Peter is usually presented without patronymic, as if he created and legitimated himself. Painted no more than three decades apart—Tsar Alexis's is the first portrait of a reigning tsar—these two portraits reflect the profound changes already under way in Russia and portend the still more dramatic transformations to follow, which would permanently alter the course of Russia's history.

Building on the innovations of his predecessors, but accelerating and expanding them dramatically through the force of his own will, Tsar Peter's responses to the challenges facing Russia would influence it far into the future. Born on May 30, 1672 (the year 7180 as Russians then reckoned time), Peter came of age in a time of cut-throat European power politics. In the early fifteenth century, Portuguese ships set sail from Lisbon and dropped anchor at a North African port, inaugurating the age of overseas empire. This brought relentless pursuit of territorial expansion both at home and abroad for the sake of economic gain and strategic security. By the seventeenth century, a state's success rested not only on its ability to mount effective fighting forces on land and sea, but

A naturalistic portrait of a living person, Tsar Alexis Mikhailovich, this painting shows the influence on Muscovy of Western visual culture and Renaissance humanism. But the portrait also evokes the past, because Alexis appears in the guise of a Byzantine emperor, thereby emphasizing Muscovy's place as rightful successor to Byzantium. Courtesy of the Slavic and Baltic Divisions, the New York Public Library, Astor, Lenox and Tilden Foundations.

equally on its capacity to mobilize the human and natural resources and obtain the financial wherewithal essential to sustaining those forces.

Despite Russia's military modernization and successes against its western foes, at the end of the seventeenth century it continued to be vulnerable. Its extended frontiers increased its exposure to potentially hostile neighbors—especially Sweden to its north—while the steppe

Painted by Godfrey Kneller in 1698 while Peter the Great was visiting London on his "Grand Embassy," this is the first official portrait of a Russian ruler. On his return to Russia, Peter introduced a revolution in artistic imagery, importing European paintings for his personal collection, recruiting European artists to teach Russian students, and sending students abroad to study painting. Supplied by Royal Collection Trust/ copyright HM Queen Elizabeth II 2014.

nomads to the south continued to raid frontier outposts and occasionally penetrate Russia's southern defenses, attacking interior towns. Russia was also economically vulnerable. It was at risk of becoming an economic colony of the West. It was dependent on foreign ships to conduct its trade through its only port at Arkhangelsk, frozen for much of the year; on European manufacturers for most for its modern weaponry; and on foreign officers and experts for the new techniques of warfare.

Russia's vulnerabilities, particularly in relation to European neighbors and trading partners, were due in part to its relatively superficial exposure to the scientific revolution and age of reason, which had begun to alter the ways that well-educated Europeans (still a minority, to be sure) regarded the natural world, and rulers managed their domains. Empirical observation and experimentation had led to major scientific discoveries and produced new technologies of obvious benefit to human beings such as the microscope, the thermometer, the barometer, and the pendulum clock. This encouraged some to believe that similar techniques might be applied to the human realm, too. Knowledge—of geography, of social life and customs, of natural resources and more— gained new significance, as rulers sought to utilize their natural and human resources more fully in pursuit of a newly important "good of the state." Yet, although Alexis and a few members of the elite were fascinated by telescopes and other imported curiosities, for most of the seventeenth century Russia even lacked schools.

During the course of his tumultuous reign, Tsar Peter strove to catch up with the West on these and other fronts. He made Europe the decisive influence on Russia, accelerating the earlier trend. European absolutist states provided the model, while social utility, worldly glory, and the good of the state displaced his subjects' salvation as the rationale for rule. Whether or not the changes he instituted were revolutionary, in the sense of being fundamentally different from what had gone before, or only an intensification of earlier developments remains a matter of heated debate among historians. However, of one thing there is little doubt: much of what transpired during his reign involved the sheer force of the ruler's own will, which left its stamp on almost everything he accomplished.

Literally a giant of a man, close to seven feet tall, Peter the Great towered over his contemporaries and displayed a restless energy and appetites to match his size. By the time he assumed power, first in 1689 as co-ruler with his half-brother Ivan, then in 1696 as sole ruler after Ivan's death, his character and tastes were fully formed and evident. Peter's impatience with the elaborate rituals that surrounded Russia's rulers distinguished him from his predecessors, as did his boundless curiosity about everything Western and his willingness to get his hands dirty. "See, brother, I'm tsar and I have a callus on my hands," he once declared.[1]

The military was his first love. During the regency of his half-sister, Sophia, Peter devoted himself to learning soldiering from the bottom up. In the 1680s, he formed "play regiments" modeled on the new-formation infantry regiments introduced into Russia decades before. Composed of local lads and courtiers, the troops drilled and even staged real battles, led by experienced foreign officers whom Peter recruited for this purpose. By the time Peter displaced Sophia, in 1689, these "play regiments" had become the effective and loyal Preobrazhensky and Semenovsky palace guard, and he, a skillful commander and soldier. A related passion was sailing, which had also interested his father. With his own hands, Peter built a "toy" fleet and then took part in constructing a war fleet that was successfully deployed against the Ottoman Turks at Azov in 1696. This, Russia's first navy, was Peter's pet project, a particular point of pride. By 1720, the navy had become numerically superior to the navies of the Swedes and Danes.

These interests drew Peter to the nearby German quarter of Moscow, where he probably learned to speak Dutch, becoming the first Russian ruler known to have mastered a foreign language. In the German quarter he found not only the technical knowledge and skilled personnel he sought but also an informality that he craved, drinking companions and compliant women. Hoping to rein him in and ensure production of an heir, in January 1690 his mother arranged his marriage to Eudokia Lopukhina, who was conventionally raised and from a minor noble clan. Although Eudokia soon became pregnant and bore a son, Alexis, in February 1690, she failed to distract her husband from his favorite pastimes.

In March 1697, Tsar Peter became the first Russian ruler to visit western Europe, incognito as the ordinary (if extraordinarily tall!) Peter Mikhailov, a member of a "Great Embassy" of some 250 men. The ostensible aim was to win allies for the struggle against the Ottoman Empire by paying courtesy calls on friendly European rulers. However, as was evident from the first major stop, the Dutch Republic, the young ruler also intended this as his voyage of discovery. As Peter Mikhailov, the (barely) disguised ruler completed studies in shipbuilding and navigation in Amsterdam and London. During the tour, which lasted eighteen months, cut short by an uprising of *streltsy* (musketeers), Peter succeeded in recruiting for service in Russia hundreds of shipwrights, naval officers, and seaman, and buying tons of naval stores. He also peered through microscopes, dissected corpses, and acquired a set of dental pliers that he loved to use on his courtiers. He came to appreciate the immense distance Russia would have to travel to catch up with the West.

Changes large and small commenced immediately after the tsar's return. The following day, he whipped out a razor and "plied [it] promiscuously among the beards" of the men who had come to greet him, leaving them as clean-shaven as himself, reported a secretary of the Austrian legation at his court.[2] A decree of 1699 altered Russia's calendar to conform to that of western Europe, starting January 1700. Another, issued in 1701, mandated "German clothes and hats and footwear" for men and women of "all ranks of the service nobility, leading merchants, military personnel, and inhabitants of Moscow and other towns," requiring of the many what a few had formerly done by choice. Only clergy and peasants were exempt.[3] A decree of 1705 commanded urban men to shave their beards and mustaches, again excluding clergy and peasants, although the latter, when bearded, were taxed whenever they came to town. More fundamental changes followed.

No man, not even one as powerful and determined as Peter the Great, could accomplish the gargantuan task of Westernizing Russia by himself. He required "new men" who shared his vision and possessed the ability and will to help implement it. It was not difficult to find them. Many of his new men derived from the old Muscovite elite, already drawn to Western ways or inspired by his vision of a resurgent Russia. Others were of foreign birth, like the Genevan Swiss officer Francois LeFort, denizen of the German quarter, who introduced Peter to foreign soldiers and merchants. Peter's "toy soldiers" supplied many more. No one became closer to the tsar than the humbly born and, so far as we know, completely illiterate Aleksandr Menshikov, rumored to have met Peter while selling pies. The two quickly became inseparable. Menshikov joined one of Peter's "play" regiments, then accompanied the ruler abroad, laboring alongside him in the docks of Amsterdam and London. Thoroughly loyal to the tsar, a gifted and courageous military commander and energetic and able organizer, Menshikov enjoyed a meteoric rise and received the highest military and civil honors. As vain and greedy as he was able, he became one of the wealthiest and most powerful men in Russia. His palace in St. Petersburg was the most luxurious of its time. It was far more extravagant than the ruler's own dwelling.

Other new men had to be created. Education provided the primary means—much, although not all of it, practical in orientation. Peter's new men were to be literate and numerate, possessing skills appropriate to their position and capacities.[4] Throughout his reign, Peter sent scores of Russians to study abroad. Some, humbly born, learned the arts of seamanship in the shipyards of London, Venice, and Amsterdam. Hundreds, however, were of noble birth, destined to supplant foreign commanders in Russia's army and navy. Russians seemed to be almost everywhere. In 1719, the nobleman Ivan Neplyuev, on his way to Spain after studying in Venice, encountered two Russians, the Nikitin brothers, studying painting in Florence, Italy; in the French port city of Toulon, he found a whole group of "high born nobles," who were learning navigation, engineering, artillery, shipbuilding, and the like, as well as dancing, fencing, and horseback riding. In Neplyuev's opinion, the last three were a waste of time, "of no use in the service of His Majesty."[5]

New schools at home also prepared new men. Most were technical in orientation, such as the Preobrazhensky guards school, founded in 1698, which taught arithmetic, geography, fortification, and artillery. Among the most significant was the Moscow School of Mathematics and Navigation, which Peter founded in 1701 on English advice, and for which he recruited two British teachers. That school and its successor, the Naval Academy, produced Russia's first generation of scientifically trained and scientifically minded individuals. As explorers, astronomers, and cartographers, its graduates would subsequently explore, measure, and map Russia's topography and identify and classify its animal, mineral, and human resources, transforming the ways that Russia's rulers conceived their empire. To crown this educational edifice, and following the example of other monarchies, Peter initiated an Academy of Sciences to serve both as a research institution and a school for advanced studies. It opened in 1725, the year of his death. Sophisticated at the top, Peter's school system was notably thin on the ground. Providing rudimentary education to young boys, it included cipher schools, decreed in 1714, which soon merged with garrison schools, and diocesan schools, staffed by the church. All were poorly funded and served few students—perhaps 4,500 by the time of Peter's death, in an empire with a population of roughly 7.78 million male "souls."

Peter's new men required new women. Soon after returning from the West, he ordered women of the court to socialize in public at European-style evening parties. Although Sophia had appeared in public ceremonies, the secretary to the Austrian legation observed in his diary that the evening parties were "a great departure from Russian manners, which up to this time forbade the female sex from appearing at public assemblies of men, and from festive gaieties."[6] Squeezed into corsets and displaying their bodies in low-cut gowns, women were expected to perform Western dances and to display appropriate social skills. Many found this change from Muscovite modesty unsettling, at least initially: "In my old age," complained the thirty-one-year-old

Daria Golitsyna, "I was reduced to showing my hair, arms and uncovered bosom to all of MOSCOW."[7] However, by the time that Peter issued his 1718 decree on assemblies, requiring that these entertainments extend beyond the court, urban elites had adopted them voluntarily. Peter even proposed sending women to Germany to finish their education, but retreated in the face of fierce noble opposition.

Peter's second wife, who took the name Catherine when she converted to Orthodoxy, was very much a new woman. Notable for her ability to keep her husband's pace, she accompanied Peter on military campaigns and diplomatic trips and shared his amusements. No one is certain about her background or religion, probably Lutheran, or even her original name, perhaps Martha. There is no doubt, however, about her humble birth and foreign origin. She came to Peter's attention in 1703 and became his mistress, bearing him a child in 1706. Having forced his first wife Eudokia into a nunnery in 1699, Peter married Catherine in 1712 after she had borne him several more children. Theirs was a new kind of wedding, conducted in the spirit of the new era. It featured ladies wearing low-cut gowns and elaborate French wigs sitting in a room with men garbed in uniform. Theirs was also a new kind of relationship—judging not by the depth of feeling, which is impossible to know from outward appearances, but by how those feelings were displayed. Whereas Muscovite culture emphasized sexual restraint and chastity, Peter loved his wife passionately and made no secret of his feelings. Portraits of the two, together with their children, became the first family portraits in Russia. In 1724, Peter crowned his wife empress.

Nothing, however, was more important to Peter than his military. It provided the means not only to defend Russia from attack but also to fulfill an imperial vision that expanded over time. During his reign, Russia was relentlessly at war. In addition to constant skirmishes along the steppe frontier with various Tatar tribes, remnants of the Golden Horde, Russia also fought wars with the Crimean Tatars' suzerains, the Ottoman Turks (1695, 1696, and 1711), with the Persians (1722–24), and most demanding of all, with Sweden (the Great Northern War, 1700–21). Peter's extended wars against numerous foes over such a lengthy front involved more intensive mobilization of human and natural resources than any previous Russian ruler had ever managed. Like other contemporary European rulers, Peter sought to remove all impediments to the exercise of his monarchical authority. He confronted far fewer obstacles than they, however—primarily the boyar duma, which he ceased to convene, and the church, whose powers and privileges he steadily eroded. Everyone, himself included, would have to serve the state. Requiring service to the state, an abstract entity, rather than to himself as tsar, represented another break with the past.

Peasant serfs, long the mainstay of Russia's armies, bore the brunt of the endless warfare. To fulfill the never-ending need for soldiers, recruitment became both more regularized and more arbitrary. After 1705, every twenty households of the tax-paying population (not only serfs but also urban artisans and laborers) were formally required to provide one recruit yearly, but additional levies were routinely imposed. In all, some 300,000 men were conscripted in the twenty years preceding Peter's death. "What sort of tsar is it who destroys the peasants' homes, takes our husbands for soldiers and leaves us orphaned with our children and forces us to weep for an age?" a peasant woman complained.[8] Unless they became disabled, soldiers served for life. The Russian army became the only entirely conscripted army in Europe (other armies included mercenaries) until the French created their revolutionary "citizens' army" at the close of the century.

Peasant serfs also provided almost all of the revenue needed to purchase armaments; pay soldiers, however minimally; and provide them with uniforms. Taxes increased, initially by expanding the items subject to direct taxation to include oak coffins, beehives, mills, fisheries, and much, much more. In 1724, a new system for taxing the peasantry replaced the most recent method, the household tax, as well as the itemized taxes. The "soul" tax, levied on every peasant male, subsumed into the tax-paying peasantry groups that had formerly enjoyed a different status, such as slaves (about 10 percent of the population). Although the peasants were burdened as never before, the lives of most nevertheless remained in many ways unchanged. Those lucky enough to escape military conscription, labor levies, or assignment to newly built factories tilled their allotments of land, chose their own elders, and enjoyed the right to enter into contracts with outsiders. While the new tax system enhanced the power of serf owners, holding them responsible for tax collecting and requiring their written permission for peasants to leave the village, peasants' collective responsibility for taxes persisted.

The provincial nobility, too, having grown accustomed to fewer service responsibilities, became subject to onerous new duties, often deeply resented. Peter required from them lifelong service, mainly military service—starting in the ranks, no less, until they earned their officer's stripes—in the guards with other nobles for the fortunate, otherwise in the infantry alongside ordinary soldiers. Leaves were rare and generally short. Commissions had to be earned, however blue a noble's blood. To ensure that nobles obtained the requisite knowledge and skills, education became compulsory for the first time in 1714, starting at the age of ten and concluding with assignment to a regiment at fifteen. Nobles who failed to complete their education were forbidden to marry. These initiatives were in many respects comparable to efforts to professionalize the military under way elsewhere in Europe. However, because Russian nobles lacked the traditional privileges of their counterparts in England, the German states, or France, Peter enjoyed greater flexibility than other rulers to impose new obligations.

In 1722, the Table of Ranks, largely modeled on the Swedish system, formalized the link between service to the state and social status. Making promotion dependent on merit and length of service, the Table opened the door for commoners (serfs excluded) to work their way up the military, civil, or court service hierarchy. If they reached the rank of major or the equivalent, they could earn nobility not only for themselves but also for their descendants. In the words of the Table: "All Russians or foreign servitors who are or actually were in the first eight ranks, their legitimate children and descendants in perpetuity, are to be considered equal to the best old Nobility though they might be of low birth."[9] Although nobles retained their privileges, they resented the potential competition from upstarts and dilution of their social status.

Merchants, too, found themselves compelled to do new things in new ways. In addition to meeting Russia's military needs and gaining independence from European suppliers, Peter also aspired to increase his people's productive capacities. He oversaw a massive increase in Russian manufacturing and required the country's merchants—accustomed to trade, not production—to play a central role. At his command, factories were constructed; merchants entrusted, even ordered, to manage them; and peasants conscripted as laborers. In 1721, a decree formally permitted merchants to purchase peasant villages for factory labor, breaking the monopoly on serf ownership of nobles, bishoprics, and monasteries. The state was the primary customer for the weapons, ammunition, and uniforms these enterprises produced. New mines were developed, in the Urals especially; older ones were expanded; and all were put under the control of the state and supplied with peasant laborers. To facilitate commerce, roads were built or improved and canals dug, once again by conscript labor. By Peter's death, roughly 200 factories existed where perhaps a dozen had been before, and Russia had become the largest producer of iron in Europe.

These measures bore tangible fruit. In 1696, Russia captured from the Turks the fortress of Azov, taking another step in the quest for access to the fertile lands of Ukraine and the Black Sea. To recover access to the Baltic, lost in the sixteenth and seventeenth centuries, Peter initiated a war with Sweden in August 1700, together with Saxon, Polish, and Danish allies. Peter anticipated an easy victory; instead, the Swedes annihilated the Russian army at Narva. Nine years later, in June 1709, Peter led his troops to victory at Poltava, barely escaping with his life when a bullet pierced his hat. Although the war dragged on for another decade, in the course of which the Turks recovered Azov (1711), the victory at Poltava represented its turning point. Duly celebrated as Russia's first national holiday, Poltava established Russia's domination of the eastern Baltic coast and displacement of Sweden as the leading power in northern Europe. When, in 1721, the Treaty of Nystad formally ended the war, Russia gained Swedish Livonia, Estonia, and Ingria; coastal islands; and the prize city of Riga. In recognition of the victory, Peter had himself crowned "Imperator [Emperor] of All Russias." The use of the foreign, Latin-based term Imperator signaled something new: the recasting of the Russian state as not simply an empire but a European empire.

Other changes followed, the most far-reaching involving the Russian Orthodox Church. In 1718, Peter commissioned the Russian-Ukrainian cleric Feofan Prokopovich to compose a new set of rules to govern it. Humbly born, unusually well educated and traveled for a cleric—he had spent time in Rome, and converted to Catholicism before reverting to Russian Orthodoxy—Prokopovich was a man of broad intellectual interests that extended far beyond theology to include mathematics, science, and literature. More unusually still, and in contrast to earlier ecclesiastical ideologues, he frequently and vocally supported the new, secular justification for the power and glory of the tsar. He became a kind of chief ideologist of the Petrine state.

Prokopovich's labors produced the Ecclesiastic Regulations, promulgated in 1721. They further curtailed the traditional autonomy and privileges of the clergy and church, and incorporated church revenues into the state budget. The patriarchate, unoccupied since 1700, was abolished and replaced by a governing board, the Holy Synod, composed of senior churchmen whom the ruler appointed. The Regulations raised the requirements for clerical education and assigned clerics new responsibilities such as registering births, marriages, and deaths and reporting signs of dissidence to the relevant state authorities. The oath required of clerics, modeled on the oath of state servitors, clearly demonstrated a new subordination of church to state and religious goals to secular ones:

I swear by Almighty God that I wish to be, as I am duty bound to be, a loyal, true, obedient and devoted servant of my natural and true

> Tsar and Sovereign Peter the First, All-Russian Autocrat, etc.... All powers, rights and prerogatives belonging to the Supreme Sovereignty of His Majesty the Tsar ... I shall guard and defend unsparingly, to the utmost limits of mind and body, even unto death should events so require.[10]

The secularization of church lands under Catherine the Great, forty years later, would make the church even more dependent on the state.

The city of St. Petersburg cast in stone the newly Europeanized face of Russia. It began as a fortress constructed on land wrested from Sweden in 1703, near the mouth of the Neva River. Peter's vision soon grew more ambitious. This would be a planned city, built from scratch along new and "modern" lines, and entirely different from "medieval" Moscow, with its narrow, winding streets and wooden houses. Peter recruited hundreds of foreign architects to design and supervise construction of palaces and government buildings made of stone in the Western style, and hundreds of painters and sculptors to decorate them. Yearly, tens of thousands of workmen were commandeered from all over Russia to perform the necessary labor. The city, Peter's "paradise," was to be beautiful as well as useful. It would boast exotic plants, trees, and gardens as well as elegant and modern buildings. Its avenues would be straight, the vistas clear; its canals as lovely as those Peter had seen in Amsterdam and Venice.

Yet apart from Peter and those close to him, few people wanted to live in the new city, at least initially, because of the cold climate, marshy soil, and expense of constructing new homes. Many nobles settled there unwillingly, by tsarist fiat, even though the better sections boasted streetlights. Merchants were at least as reluctant. Seeking to make St. Petersburg Russia's chief port on the basis of its access to the Baltic and lengthier freedom from ice, Peter pressed merchants to route their trade through Petersburg rather than Arkhangelsk, only to encounter foot-dragging. Nevertheless, after 1709, when the victory at Poltava eliminated the Swedish threat, the city gradually became Russia's new capital, officially in 1713. Over time, it also became Russia's largest port and a center of international commerce, her "window on the West."

The rapid appearance of so many foreign objects, institutions, and persons; the offenses against hallowed traditions; and the burden of taxes, recruitment, and compulsory labor that demanded so much from people who gained nothing tangible in return inevitably generated opposition. Some became convinced that Peter was the anti-Christ, or

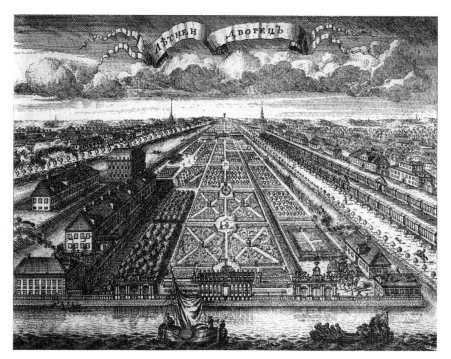

Aleksei Zubov completed this engraving of St. Petersburg's Summer Palace and its garden in 1717. Like other contemporary images of the city, it reflects an ideal of orderliness and symmetry rather than the more complex and messy reality. The State Hermitage Museum, St. Petersburg.

a foreign foundling who had been exchanged for the real ruler. Many, not only peasant serfs but nobles, too, simply fled to the southern or eastern borderlands of Russia to escape the new demands. Clergymen protested foreign influences. Popular unrest peppered Peter's reign. The Don Cossack Ataman Kondratii Bulavin led the most threatening rebellion in 1707. It garnered support from other Cossacks as well as Russian laborers and took nine months to suppress.

The greatest challenge to Peter's vision, however, derived from his own son, Alexis. Born to Peter's first wife, Alexis was raised by Eudokia and her relatives until Peter divorced her by forcing her into a nunnery. The heir to the throne disappointed his father in every way imaginable: he was indifferent to military matters and hostile to Western innovations. He preferred his Finnish peasant mistress to his wife, Charlotte of Wolfenbüttel; preferred Moscow to St. Petersburg; and lent a willing ear to people who disliked his father's ways. A clash between willful father and reluctant son was virtually inevitable. In 1715, after Charlotte and Catherine both gave birth to sons, Alexis was pressed to give up the throne and fled to Vienna with his mistress, seeking asylum. He was lured back, then accused of conspiring with the Austrians to overthrow and assassinate Peter. To compel him to name his supposed accomplices, Alexis was subjected to torture, which was routine in those days. In late June 1718, he died, perhaps as a result. Four years later, Peter promulgated Russia's first law of succession. Allowing the reigning sovereign to designate whomever he chose as heir, it flew in the face of a fundamental law of hereditary monarchy.[11]

Then, in 1725, Peter himself died, having named no heir. He left an exhausted nation, its peasantry bled dry. He had achieved his goal of placing Russia on the map of Europe, however. By the time of Peter's death, Russia had become a full member of the European state system. For the first time, Russian embassies existed in the capitals of Europe, with ambassadors who dressed like their European counterparts, conducted themselves appropriately, and were often fluent in the local language. Russians of the ruling family now married German spouses, as Alexis had, and as did Peter's nieces, the daughters of his late brother Ivan: Anna to the Duke of Courland and Catherine to the Duke of Mecklenburg. In northern Europe, Russia had become the foremost power, without whom no major question involving European policy could be decided. Maps of Europe, drawn not only in Russia but elsewhere, would subsequently locate the boundary dividing Europe from Asia at the Ural Mountains rather than along the Don River as previously.

Eulogizing Peter after his death, Feofan Prokopovich celebrated him in characteristically glowing terms. Ignoring the accomplishments of Peter's predecessors and exaggerating those of Peter himself, Prokopovich declared:

> What manner of man did we lose? He was your Samson, Russia.... He found but little strength in you, and on the model of his name he made your power strong like a rock and diamond. Finding an army that was disorderly at home, weak in the field, the butt of the enemies' derision, he created one that was useful to the fatherland, terrible to the enemy, renowned and glorious everywhere. In defending the fatherland, he at the same time returned to it lands that had been wrested from it and augmented it by the acquisition of new provinces.... Oh Russia, he was your Solomon, who received from the Lord reason and wisdom in great plenty. This is proven by the manifold philosophic disciplines introduced by him

and his showing and imparting to many of his subjects the knowledge of a variety of inventions and crafts unknown to us before his time.... We see and marvel, then, at our fatherland; it has changed externally and internally, and become immeasurably better than it had been previously. [12]

And yet, these exaggerations also contain real truth. The question is, how much? On that, historians continue to differ, while Russians still debate the question of whether Peter's innovations were really needed, beneficial in the long term and the short, or worth the price they exacted from Russia's people.

CHAPTER 5

The Triumph of Empire
(1725–1855)

In the late 1760s, on a small estate outside the mining town of Ekaterinburg a thousand miles east of St. Petersburg, the thirteen-year-old Anna Yakovleva watched as her widowed mother, a noblewoman, prepared a feast. They awaited a visit from Bashkir tribesmen, semi-nomadic Muslims who often attacked settlers like the Yakovlevs to drive them from the Bashkir's ancestral pasturelands. "I shall not depart from any place that God has given me," Yakovleva assured her daughter. To her Bashkir guests, Yakovleva declared: "I have no other protector except God, whom you know as well." Touched by Yakovleva's pleas and tamed by her Christian charity as her daughter tells the story, the Bashkirs departed after having eaten and drunk their fill, promising to be Yakovleva's protectors and not her enemies.[1]

Russia's empire, proclaimed by Peter the Great early in the century, had expanded dramatically by its end. New peoples came under Russian dominion; Russian settlers often followed, colonizing their land. The recently strengthened military finally vanquished the pastoral peoples— remnants of the former Mongol hordes, who had for centuries threatened inhabitants of the forested interior—thereby securing and extending Russia's frontiers. Russia's annexation of the North Caucasus was well under way. Victory over the Ottoman Empire in two wars (1768–74, 1788–1792) secured the territory north of the Black Sea as far west as the Dniester River, including the vital agricultural and mineral resources of southern Ukraine, an area that became known as New Russia. In the process, Russia annexed the Crimea in 1783. Three partitions of Poland (1772, 1793, and 1795), undertaken in concert with Prussia and Austria, consolidated Russia's domination of the eastern Baltic and added more than seven million new subjects to her realm. Those subjects included, for the first time, a substantial minority of Jews. Russia's empire extended almost exclusively over land, unlike the empires of western Europe, but in 1784 it laid claim to Kodiak Island off the coast of Alaska. Russia's elites took enormous pride in an empire that by the end of the eighteenth century encompassed an astounding variety of peoples, languages, cultures, and faiths, and was exceeded in size only by the British Empire.

Catherine the Great, the most powerful female ruler in the history of Europe, presided over this culmination of Peter the Great's imperial initiatives. She positioned herself as a worthy successor to Peter in other ways as well. She not only greatly furthered the Westernizing tendencies that Peter had promoted but also substantially enhanced Russia's role in European power politics, a role her immediate successors would act to preserve. For Catherine, these achievements provided a source of legitimacy as well as pride.

Catherine had seized the throne by force. Born Sophia Augusta in 1729 in a small German principality, the future Catherine the Great came to Russia in 1744 to marry Peter III, the legitimate heir. She learned Russian, converted to Orthodoxy, took the name Ekaterina Alekseevna (Catherine), and married Peter seventeen months later. The marriage proved unhappy and, likely, unconsummated. Marginalized at court, threatened by banishment to a nunnery to free Peter to marry his mistress, Catherine spent her time reading widely in Enlightenment literature and cultivating friends in key places. Six months after Peter III ascended the throne, Catherine ousted him in a coup d'état, assisted by her lover, Grigorii Orlov. The Guards regiments, composed of the cream of the nobility, immediately recognized her as Russia's ruler. The next day, she and her friend Princess Ekaterina Dashkova rode out at the head of troops and arrested Peter, who died under mysterious circumstances a few days later. Catherine then proceeded to the Kazan Cathedral in St. Petersburg, where the church hierarchy proclaimed her ruler.

Catherine's coup marked the fourth time since the death of Peter the Great that the Guards regiments figured prominently in the ascension of Russia's rulers. All were female: Catherine I, Peter's widow (reigned 1725–27); Anna, Peter's niece (1730–40); Elizabeth, his daughter (1741–61), and Catherine II (The Great), who ruled until 1796. To make female rule palatable to a conservative public, the empresses were presented as powerful yet disarmingly mild and loving figures, showering their bounty on their people. Presenting Catherine's coup as a bloodless, popular revolution, Dashkova described its reception: "Countless people thronged the streets shouting and screaming, invoking blessings upon us and giving vent to their joy in countless ways, while the old and

0 200 mi

0 300 km

Barents Sea

White Sea

Arkhangelsk

FINLAND

Karelia

Gulf of Finland   St. Petersburg

Ingria

Estonia

Novgorod

Livonia

Riga

RUSSIA

Volga River

Moscow

Baltic Sea

POLAND
(1815)

Dnieper River

Ukraine

Dniester River

BESSARABIA

Crimea

Don River

Volga River

Danube River

Black Sea

RUSSIAN EXPANSION
IN EUROPE,
1689–1825

☐ Acquired by Peter the Great,
1689–1725

▨ Acquired between 1730–1762

▨ Acquired by Catherine the Great,
1762–1795

▨ Partitions of Poland, 1772–1795

▨ Acquired by Alexander I,
1801–1825

OTTOMAN EMPIRE

the sick were held up at open windows by their children to enable them to see with their own eyes the triumph that shone on everyone's face."[2] Such personal devotion to Catherine became an important motif of her reign. It supposedly united with the throne not only Russians but also the empire's diverse peoples. Catherine herself delighted in the complete listing of her title, which enumerated the many provinces and lands under her rule, including the newly conquered regions.

Imagery notwithstanding, the primary recipients of the empresses' bounty were nobles. After Peter the Great's death, the requirement that nobles serve the state was gradually eased; increasingly, nobles resembled a privileged class. Nobles monopolized the highest positions in the imperial administration and enjoyed the privilege of early enrollment in service and more rapid advancement, despite the Table of Ranks. In 1761, nobles' service requirement was abolished altogether. Catherine confirmed the abolition, and included it in her Charter of the Nobility of 1785, which also affirmed nobles' immunity from corporal punishment and sole right to possess serfs. The Charter established nobles as the first in Russia to have legally defined rights as a group. The highest strata of native peoples in newly conquered territories gained these rights as well, due to Russia's long-standing policy of assimilating them into the nobility. German aristocrats from the Baltic provinces, Tatar aristocrats from the Crimea, Polish nobles from the partitioned lands, and the upper strata of the Don and Zaporozhets Cossacks joined Russia's system of power and privilege.

Culture flourished during Catherine's reign, very much influenced by ideas emanating from the West. The empress herself was a prolific writer. She founded Russia's first satirical journal, authored works in a variety of genres, and corresponded with prominent Enlightenment figures such as Diderot and Voltaire. Nobles also developed intellectual interests, encouraged by the new freedom from compulsory service. Andrei Bolotov was one of them. Enrolled in his father's regiment at the age of ten, Bolotov retired from service fifteen years later in 1763. He returned to his rural estate south of Moscow, bearing books on agronomy he had purchased while stationed in East Prussia. After remodeling his estate according to contemporary ideas of science and civilization, Bolotov devoted himself to landscape gardening and agricultural improvement, detailing his discoveries in contemporary journals and newspapers.

Such writings served a reading public that had grown dramatically in size by the final decades of the century, while remaining a small island of Europeanized culture in a sea of popular illiteracy. In the major cities, public life grew livelier. Clubs, coffeehouses, and salons offered the leisured opportunities to socialize and exchange ideas, much as they did elsewhere Europe. Theater grew popular, not only in cities but sometimes even in the remote provinces, where nobles with sufficient means might remove dozens of serfs from fieldwork—some 2,000 serfs between 1770 and 1820—to train as musicians, singers, dancers, and actors. New journals appeared, especially after Catherine permitted private presses for the first time. Most members of the reading public were nobles, educated at home or at boarding school. In 1764, when Catherine founded the Smolny Institute for Girls of Noble Birth, formal education became available to noblewomen, too.

The remarkable Mikhail Lomonosov represents a significant exception to noble predominance in intellectual life. The son of a prosperous peasant who owned merchant and fishing vessels near the White Sea, Lomonosov was a self-made man. Taught to read by a neighbor, in 1731, at the age of nineteen, he made his way to Moscow and enrolled in the Slavic Greek Latin Academy. Because the Academy barred peasants, he claimed to be the son of a nobleman, and then performed so well that he was allowed to remain even after the authorities discovered his falsehood. Thereafter, he was sent to study at the Academy of Sciences, Russia's premier educational institution, and then to the University of Marburg. A polymath—poet, historian, astronomer, physicist, and chemist—in 1755 Lomonosov produced a grammar that regularized Russia's language and cleared a path for future writers.

Much of Russia's newly vibrant culture was sustained by the labor of peasant serfs. Some 55 percent of them belonged to nobles. Over the course of the eighteenth century, privately owned serfs lost rights they once enjoyed, transforming their status into something very like slavery. Although most serfs still tilled their own allotment of land and governed their own villages, their noble masters otherwise enjoyed near total power over them, at least formally. Nobles could do just about anything they wanted with their serfs, short of deliberate murder. They could move serfs where they pleased; buy and sell them individually and without land; give them as gifts or remove them from the fields to do housework or perform for owners' amusement. Serfs who worked land in the fertile south fared worst. There, profitable farming encouraged noble serf owners to intensify exploitation. Surplus grain could be shipped north and sold in the Russian heartland or exported for sale to Europe after trade through the Black Sea grew more secure. Pursuit of profit led nobles to increase their holdings at the expense of peasant allotments, require peasants to neglect their own fields and cultivate those of the nobles, and harshly punish peasants who failed to maintain proper discipline.

The mostly nomadic inhabitants of the highly fertile southern steppe fared no better. For them, Russian conquest meant disruptive change. Brutally suppressing local resistance, the state offered incentives to settlers, foreign as well as Russian, to occupy and transform native pasturelands into productive farms. Within a few decades, some half a million colonists, roughly 20 percent of them foreign, had taken up the offer. Foreigners included Albanians, Greeks, French, Swedes, and nearly 30,000 Germans. This settlement policy delivered the final blow to the Kalmyks, Buddhist Mongols who had occupied the Caspian steppe in the seventeenth century and who were already weakened by Russia's presence in the region. In 1771, more than 150,000 Kalmyks abandoned their pasturelands and fled eastward.

The Russian state's encroachment on the lives of formerly free peoples, the intensification of serfdom, Westernizing changes, and more contributed to the largest popular revolt in Russia's history. It began in 1773, with another in Russia's long history of pretenders, this time a Yaik Cossack named Emelyan Pugachev. Claiming to be the legitimate ruler, Peter III, he roused fellow Cossacks to rebellion with promises to oust the foreign usurper, Catherine, and restore an idealized version of life before Peter the Great. Pugachev quickly attracted a massive following. Old Believers flocked to his side. Bashkirs provided some of his most loyal supporters. In the Ural Mountains, factory serfs supplied his forces with weapons and ammunition. Millions of serfs heeded his summons to rise up against their owners:

> We free all those formerly oppressed by the villainous nobles and bribe-takers and judges, all peasants and all the people oppressed by obligations and burdens.... [As for] those who hitherto were nobles, with their estates, those opponents of our power and disruptors of the empire and ruiners of peasants, catch, kill, and hang them, and treat them just as they, having no Christianity, treated you, the peasants.[3]

Soon, the entire south was ablaze in rebellion. Before Russian troops finally managed to quell the revolt in 1775, it briefly engulfed the city of Kazan and threatened Moscow. A terrifying experience that cost thousands of nobles their lives, the Pugachev uprising came to exemplify the threat of popular revolt to Russia's ruling classes. Bolotov, present at Pugachev's public execution, observed it with relief.

The revolution that erupted in 1789 in France presented another kind of threat, alerting Catherine and subsequent rulers to the potential danger of ideas. The French Revolution permanently altered European politics. It ended the seigneurial privileges of French nobles, replaced absolute monarchy with an elected assembly, encouraged hope for popular sovereignty, and in the Reign of Terror, took the lives of King Louis XVI, his wife Marie Antoinette, and tens of thousands of others. The revolution made Catherine more conservative, less tolerant of criticism. This sealed the fate of Aleksandr Radishchev, a minor noble and civil servant, a former student at the University of Leipzig, and one of a relative handful of thinkers to favor an end to serfdom. His book, *A Journey from St. Petersburg to Moscow*, published in 1790, offered a devastating critique of it. Perhaps worse, it strongly implied the illegitimacy of all systems of power that limited human freedom, Russia's autocratic order among them. Radishchev wrote: "But humanity will roar in its fetters, and, moved by the hope of freedom and the indestructible law of nature, will push on.... And tyranny will be dismayed. The united force of all despotism, of all oppressive power will in a moment be dispersed, o chosen of days!" Catherine was appalled, finding such language "completely revolutionary," as she noted in her own copy of the book.[4] She ordered Radishchev's arrest and the book's destruction. Sentenced to death, Radishchev was then reprieved and exiled to Siberia.

Thereafter, Russia's rulers had to reckon with both the winds of change emanating from the West and a nobility protective of their privileges. The fate of Paul I, Catherine's son and successor, offered a lesson to subsequent monarchs. Endeavoring to stop the spread of dangerous ideas, Paul restricted travel abroad, tightened censorship, and barred not only French books, as his mother had done after 1793, but even French fashions and music. He also rejected his mother's respect for noble rights. Demanding absolute deference, he ordered the flogging of nobles who displeased him. His actions violated the Charter of the Nobility and offended nobles' newly enhanced sense of dignity. Less than five years after Paul became tsar, the Guards ousted and murdered him, clearing the way for the reign of his son, Alexander, whom they found far more appealing.

Instead of avoiding Western ideas, Alexander I sought to keep abreast of Western political trends. In addition to easing censorship and ending the prohibition on foreign books and travel, Alexander initiated educational changes with far-reaching consequences. In order to recruit qualified commoners and produce trained civil servants of the sort increasingly staffing bureaucracies in the West, in 1803 and 1804 Alexander introduced a kind of educational ladder. Beginning in local schools, which were open to all males without distinction of social class except for privately owned serfs, the ladder culminated at the university.

To cap the system, five new universities were established in addition to Moscow University, founded in 1755. After 1809, having a university degree or passing a university exam became a requirement for rising to the service rank that conferred hereditary nobility. Over the following decades, Russia's bureaucracy gradually grew more professional and its members' social origins more diverse, while universities became a breeding ground for independent thought. Alexander even toyed with the notion of granting Russia a constitution. At his request, Mikhail Speransky, his most influential aide, developed a constitutional project that he presented to the tsar in 1809. The project would have established an indirectly elected legislature with limited power and subjected the tsar to the rule of law. In the end, Alexander proved unwilling to limit his own absolute authority and never implemented the Western-style constitution.

Despite his hatred of serfdom as an oppressive institution, Alexander was likewise unwilling to ease the lot of privately owned serfs. Reluctant to alienate the nobility, on whom he still depended for military and civil service, the ruler instituted no substantive changes. He merely allowed serf masters to emancipate their chattel voluntarily (1803) and permitted the emancipation of serfs without land in the Baltic provinces, a disaster for the peasants. Yet changes in serf status occurred nonetheless. They resulted from the growing economic specialization of Russia's north and south. Freed from the need to feed themselves and their owners year round by grain from the south, peasants in the heartland increasingly engaged in other pursuits such as petty trade or craft production. Or, after obtaining their owner's permission, they headed elsewhere to work for wages, a portion of which they paid as quitrent.

Some peasant serfs grew wealthy, like the parents of Savva Purlevsky, who kept two servants. Born in 1800 in a village northeast of Moscow with a long history of trading, Purlevsky learned to do business from his father. Selling flax and yarn in winter, and renting a profitable apple orchard in summer, he soon became a successful tradesman. Still, he remained a serf, helpless to resist the whims of his masters. He also hated a status that in his view, "belittle[d] me in the eyes of free people."[5] Purlevsky eventually abandoned everything to flee, illegally, to freedom in the southern borderlands. Other serf entrepreneurs stayed put. Numerous nineteenth-century merchant and entrepreneurial families originated as serfs, founding rural industries with money borrowed from wealthy masters and employing fellow serfs. Proving no barrier to the emergence of industrial capitalism in Russia, serfdom would nevertheless hamper its further development. But until lack of development led to military failure, it seemed easier to allow serfdom to persist.

Military success, however, not failure, marked the first half of the century. The triumph over Napoleon held the greatest significance for Russia's international stature and Russians' own self-image. It inspired Leo Tolstoy's great novel *War and Peace* and Peter Tchaikovsky's *1812 Overture*. When, in June 1812, Napoleon Bonaparte crossed the Nieman River with an enormous army, he brought war to the heart of Russia for the first time in two centuries. Having conquered and transformed central Europe, Napoleon anticipated an easy victory. Instead, he encountered an unorthodox but effective military strategy, a resolute ruler, and a people who appeared united against him, despite Russia's yawning social divide.

Avoiding direct combat, at which Napoleon excelled, in the face of overwhelming force Tsar Alexander authorized a policy of retreat that took advantage of Russia's vast spaces. Luring Napoleon's forces far from their base, retreating Russian forces employed a "scorched earth" tactic to deny their enemies food and fodder, then attacked their vulnerable flanks and rear. The invasion stimulated an unprecedented outpouring of patriotism. Society rallied behind the war effort: gunsmiths in Tula factories worked overtime to produce rifles; nobles volunteered to lead troops; tradesmen contributed money and goods. In November, several dozen noblewomen formed a Women's Patriotic Society. "Women, too, seek to be useful to society," its charter read.[6]

Effective in the long term, in the short term retreat appeared a national disgrace to newly awakened patriots eager for battle. Rank and file soldiers, officers, and much of the educated public equated retreat with flight. General Petr Bagration, commander of the Second Army, the son of a Georgian prince who had come to identify as a Russian, put this view succinctly: "Russians ought not to flee.... We have become worse than the Prussians."[7] Such eagerness for combat led to the colossal and inconclusive Battle of Borodino, in which nearly 100,000 men lost their lives, Bagration among them.

The following week, in mid-September, Napoleon reached Moscow. He found the city nearly deserted, its wooden buildings

This painting depicts the parting of Tsar Alexander I, who stands on a boat, and Napoleon Bonaparte, to his right on the shore, after signing the Treaty of Tilsit in July 1807, following Russia's defeat at Friedland. The treaty required Russia to recognize French control of central Europe and to support the Continental System, the boycott of British goods that aimed at breaking Britain's growing global might, but it also left Russia in command of much of eastern Europe and the only major power on the continent besides France. The State Hermitage Museum, St. Petersburg.

aflame. Napoleon spent a month trying, in vain, to make peace with Tsar Alexander, who refused to negotiate while French troops remained on Russian soil. Then Napoleon began a costly retreat. Forced by the brilliant general Mikhail Kutuzov to return along their devastated invasion route, Napoleon's men were harassed by Russian arms and by irregulars, many of them peasants. When Napoleon abandoned Russia, less than a tenth of his original troops remained. Russian forces pursued them. In alliance with Prussia, Sweden, and eventually, Austria and Great Britain, Russians fought their way across Europe and entered Paris in triumph at the end of March 1814.

This was a heady moment for both the tsar and his officer elite. Victory over Napoleon completed Russia's transformation into a preeminent European power. Only Great Britain rivaled it. Tsar Alexander became a leading actor on the European stage, the sole ruler to participate in the Congress of Vienna, where the victorious powers endeavored to restore the pre-Napoleonic balance of power in Europe. In Vienna, Alexander supported constitutions for France and the kingdom of Poland, newly incorporated into the Russian empire. But thereafter, he grew more conservative. When liberal revolutions broke out in Spain and southern Italy in 1820, he favored crushing them, in concert with Austria and Prussia. Fearful that Russia, together with other conservative powers, might even help to restore Spain's authority over its former Latin American colonies, in 1823 United States President James Monroe issued the Monroe Doctrine. It warned European conservatives to keep their hands off the American continents.

Victory over Napoleon had the opposite effect on the cream of Russia's nobility. It raised their expectations of reform at home. Through reading and discussion, many had grown familiar with liberal French ideas, while officers who had marched with Russia's armies into Paris saw with their own eyes the well-being of people free of absolute authority. Alexander's approval of constitutions for France and the Kingdom of Poland encouraged their hopes. To return from triumph abroad to serfdom and Russia's authoritarian political order at home was more than some could endure. The experience had a profound effect on the nobly born Ivan Yakushkin, a participant in the campaigns against Napoleon, as he testified in 1825: "My stay abroad during the military campaigns probably drew my attention, for the first time, to the social organization of Russia and compelled me to see its defects. After my return from abroad, serfdom seemed to me the only obstacle to the drawing together of all classes and ... to the civil reorganization of Russia."[8] Frustrated in this hope for liberal reform, Yakushkin joined a revolutionary conspiracy aimed at abolishing serfdom and establishing representative government and a constitutional order in Russia. On December 14, 1825, following Alexander's death and on the day his successor, his younger brother Nicholas, was to be crowned, conspirators staged an abortive insurrection. Government forces easily suppressed the rebellion, which became known as the Decembrist uprising. Five of the conspirators were hanged; hundreds more paid for their rebellion with a lifetime sentence of penal servitude in Siberia.

Aleksandra Muravyeva was one of scores of high-born wives who followed their exiled Decembrist husbands to Siberia after their failed uprising in 1825. Required to abandon their social privileges and to leave their children behind, the women became models of idealistic female self-sacrifice in the eyes of subsequent generations. "Women alone were not guilty of this shameful denial of their dear ones," wrote the socialist Aleksander Herzen, celebrating their courage and condemning the cowardice of aristocratic men in the face of the political repression.[10] Petr F. Sokolov, Portrait of A. G. Muravieva, the Wife of the Decembrist, *State Hermitage Museum, St. Petersburg. From* The Female Portrait in Russian Art *(Leningrad: Aurora Art Publishers, 1974).*

The rebellion and its outcome cast a pall over the reign of Russia's new ruler. Already inclined to conservatism, fanatical about order and discipline, Tsar Nicholas I attributed unrest at home and abroad to dangerous Western ideas. He devoted his thirty-year reign to combating that danger. "Orthodoxy, autocracy and nationality" became the catchwords of his rule. "Autocracy," the key term, indicated the subservience of everyone to the ruler. "Nationality" reinforced it. Based on the word *narod*, meaning the people, the term encouraged the celebration of Russian language and culture, while emphasizing the distinguishing characteristic of Russians: their voluntary subordination to their ruler. The term nationality thus reflected the broader awakening of national sentiment in post-Napoleonic Europe, while countering its democratic challenge. Censorship tightened and after 1826 became the responsibility of the notorious Third Section. A secret police organization, it was tasked with political and moral surveillance of the realm.

Everywhere it emerged, opposition met repression. When Polish nationalists rebelled in 1830, demanding independence from Russia, the tsar dispatched troops to crush them. He then abolished the Polish constitution. Popular resistance to Russia's continuing conquest of the North Caucasus was treated with still greater brutality. In their efforts to subdue its inhabitants—an unusually diverse melange of ethnic groups, including the Chechens—Russian forces committed atrocities that included rape, pillaging, and the indiscriminate slaughter of women and children. Instead of quelling resistance, these tactics managed temporarily to unify peoples with disparate customs, languages, even religious beliefs. By the 1830s, most had united under the leadership of Imam Shamil, a Sufi Muslim, in a holy war against Russia that raged until 1859, ending only with Shamil's capture. The tsar's reach also extended beyond his empire's borders. His role in suppressing the revolutions that erupted in 1848 earned Nicholas the name "Gendarme of Europe."

Yet wittingly or not, he presided over a period of cultural efflorescence, when Russian literature finally came into its own. Alexander Pushkin, Russia's most revered poet and one of its most celebrated novelists, reached the peak of his literary prowess during Nicholas's reign. Pushkin was the descendant of an African, Abram Hannibal (exact birthplace unknown), who had been presented in 1704 to Peter the Great as an exotic gift and eventually rose to become a general and a noble. Pushkin knew French almost as well as Russian and drew on a range of literary precursors while remaining beholden to none. His *Eugene Onegin*, published in serial form between 1825 and 1832, was Russia's first great novel (in verse). It featured a noble protagonist who lives a life of frivolity, kills a young friend in a duel, and spurns the love of Tatiana Larina, one of Russian literature's most attractive heroines, realizing her value only after he has lost her. Onegin became the first in a series of literary "superfluous men," alienated from Russian society but helpless to change it.

Pushkin embodied the contradictory trends of this era. Personally censored by the tsar himself because of his liberal sympathies, like many well-educated Russians Pushkin took pride in Russia's might and the empire's territorial magnitude and diversity. In a poem entitled

"Slanderers," he responded with ire to Europeans who criticized Russia's suppression of the Polish insurrection:

> Has the Russian become unused to victories?
> Or are we too few? Or
>   Won't the Russian land
> From Perm to Tavrida
> From the cold Finnish cliffs to the fiery Colchis
>   From the Shaken Kremlin
>   To the walls of motionless China
> Arise, its steel blade flashing.[9]

The *Philosophical Letters*, published in 1836, challenged such nationalist pride. Composed by Petr Chaadaev, another disillusioned veteran of the war against Napoleon, they also crystallized divergent views regarding Russia's proper course of development that can still be heard today. Comparing Russia unfavorably with the West, Chaadaev dismissed Russian culture as stagnant and backward, outside the mainstream of European developments. His challenge split intellectuals into two camps, Slavophiles and Westernizers. Slavophiles embraced, indeed celebrated, Russia's differences from western Europe, which they condemned as individualistic and materialistic. In their view, Russia possessed unique virtues such as *sobornost*, or social collectivity, as embodied in the peasant commune, which made Russia superior, not inferior, to the West. Westernizers believed the opposite: Russia resembled Europe but was more backward, needing to develop along lines similar to the West. Westernizers welcomed Peter the Great's innovations as setting Russia on the proper path; Slavophiles condemned many of his changes for betraying Russia's unique virtues.

From these opposing views, Aleksandr Herzen crafted a uniquely Russian vision of socialism. The illegitimate son of a nobleman and his German mistress, Herzen became critical of Tsar Nicholas I during his student days at Moscow University and suffered five years of exile in the provinces. Already a socialist when he left Russia in 1847, he expected change to come from the West, only to have his expectations dashed by the defeat of worker uprisings in France during the revolutions of 1848. Thereafter, Herzen came to believe that Russia offered the best hope for a socialist future. In his view, the peasant commune, with its egalitarian and communitarian practices, self-government, and lack of individualistic property relations, provided the embryo of this superior social form.

Whatever their views, Russia's educated elites were shocked by Russia's humiliating defeat in the Crimean War of 1853–56. Russia fought alone against Turkey, France, and Great Britain, the latter two eager to curtail Russia's growing strength in the region. Although none of the contenders fought well, Russia alone fought on her own turf. The war revealed all of her weaknesses. These were exacerbated by the absence of railroads, emblematic of Russia's industrial backwardness by comparison with Great Britain and France. Unable to move sufficient troops to the front, the regime was also unable to supply soldiers adequately with food and armaments once they arrived. Despite the efforts of the surgeon Nikolai Pirogov and his nurse volunteers—the counterparts of the British nurse Florence Nightingale—Russia also could not care properly for its wounded. The Treaty of Paris, signed on March 30, 1856, a year after Nicholas's death, forced Russia to accept the neutralization of the Black Sea and retrocede to Turkey the mouth of the Danube and part of Bessarabia, won from the Turks almost half a century earlier. The Crimean defeat signified the end of Russia's status as the supreme land power in Europe. It made fundamental reforms unavoidable.

CHAPTER 6

Reform and Revolution (1855–1905)

In the summer of 1857, police in rural Moscow arrived to quell a rebellion by peasant serfs. The serfs had already complained, in vain, about their abusive noble master. Now they refused to acknowledge his authority, flouted his orders, and cursed him right in front of the police. Police efforts to arrest the ringleader, Egor Pankratyev, failed when villagers tore Pankratyev from their grasp. Then, after threatening to smash officers' skulls, the rebels fled the village. During the first half of the nineteenth century, such overt serf resistance had increased dramatically. Still more serfs resisted oppressive circumstances covertly—fleeing estates, dragging their feet, withholding payments or labor. Warning of the danger of another Pugachev revolt, the feared outcome of such isolated incidents, on March 30, 1856, less than two weeks after the Crimean War ended, the new tsar, Alexander II, announced his intention to emancipate the serfs. "It is better to abolish serfdom from above than wait until it begins to abolish itself from below," he declared to a group of Moscow nobles.[1] Despite this and other far-reaching reforms, half a century later revolution from below shook the foundations of the Russian empire.

Among the reasons for reform were the Crimean debacle and the decline in Russia's international stature. Powered by capitalist industrialization, Great Britain and France (joined after 1871 by a newly unified Germany) engaged in fierce global competition for markets and resources. Many enlightened bureaucrats attributed Russia's inability to compete successfully to serfdom, which acted as a brake on economic growth. To restore Russia's status, serfdom would have to be ended—but doing so would not be easy. However compelling the reasons for emancipation, conservatives strenuously opposed it. They were determined either to prevent emancipation altogether or at least to ensure that the terms were as favorable as possible to the nobility.

Five years elapsed between the tsar's declaration and the emancipation itself, while behind closed doors a committee of officials wrestled with these conflicts.

Still, the intellectual atmosphere lightened almost immediately. Censorship eased, allowing the press for the first time to discuss the prospective emancipation. New literary journals appeared and older ones grew livelier. The ban on foreign university study, instituted under Nicholas I, was lifted, freeing students to study abroad. At home, universities ceased giving preference to nobles and capping student enrollment; they also reduced tuition fees. The student body diversified. In 1858, the tsar approved Russia's first high schools for girls, admitting students from all social backgrounds. In 1859, Jews who possessed sufficient wealth or education for the first time gained the right to settle on territory outside the Pale of Settlement that extended along the Empire's western borderlands.

The intellectual ferment was striking to a returning traveler: "When you arrive [back] in Russia you will run the risk of not recognizing it. Externally, everything seems the same, but you feel an inner renovation in everything, you feel a new era is beginning," he remarked in a letter to a friend. "Read our newspapers and journals, listen to the conversation in the brilliant salons and in modest homes, and you will be amazed at the work which these heads are accomplishing. From all sides, ideas and new perspectives are little by little displacing the old routines."[2]

Eager to participate in the regeneration of their society, the educated public anticipated far-reaching changes. Many—the men at least—also aspired to a political role in an elected, representative body such as those already sharing power with the British monarch, among others. Even more than in western Europe, where the ideas first originated, the "woman question" became one of the burning issues of the day. It involved critiques of gender relations and of women's limited educational and employment opportunities. Its more radical proponents challenged the patriarchal family itself, in which by law, husbands and fathers enjoyed near-absolute authority over wives and children. An embryonic women's movement emerged. Led by Anna Filosofova, Nadezhda Stasova, and Maria Trubnikova—well-educated women from elite backgrounds—the movement devoted itself to expanding women's employment and educational opportunities.

When it was finally promulgated on February 19, 1861, the long-awaited emancipation of the serfs, applauded by some, appeared a half-measure to others who hoped for more. Essentially transforming privately owned serfs into state peasants—who represented over half the peasant population at the time—it was a compromise, aimed at reconciling competing interests and preserving continuity amid real change. It clearly favored noble masters more than peasant serfs. Serfs did gain freedom from servitude as well as an allotment of land, unlike slaves in the southern United States, whose emancipation provided no guaranteed access to land. But peasants often received less land than they had tilled as serfs, while nobles kept the remainder. Almost as upsetting, at least from the peasants' perspective, they had to pay their former owners for the land they received, often at prices that exceeded its market value. The state provided the payments up front; peasants were required to repay the state with interest (called redemption payments) over a period up to forty-nine years.

Even freedom was limited, although many of the limitations were familiar and peasants unlikely to resent them. Peasant institutions assumed much of the authority formerly exercised by noble landowners. Peasant courts now judged peasant crimes. Peasant officials granted internal passports to potential migrants. Peasant heads of households met regularly to allocate land, taxes, and redemption payments among themselves. To avoid the formation of a landless and potentially rebellious proletariat such as that currently fueling unrest in industrialized countries, the emancipation also made it difficult for peasants to surrender their allotments and sever ties with their village. Sporadic acts of peasant resistance followed the emancipation. Met with government repression, they soon subsided. The terms of the emancipation would shape peasant life and feed peasant grievances for the next half century.

The reforms that followed—known collectively as the Great Reforms—likewise brought significant change. The university reform of 1863 set the stage for Russia's future intellectual contributions, including contributions to the global history of the natural sciences. Universities gained unprecedented freedom from state control and the right to govern their own affairs. University curricula expanded, especially in mathematics and science, and laboratory facilities greatly improved. Two years before the reform, Dmitrii Mendeleev had returned to St. Petersburg from studying the new field of modern chemistry abroad, mostly in Heidelberg. In 1868, having successfully defended his dissertation and become a full professor at St. Petersburg University, Mendeleev presented the world with the basis of the periodic table, the periodic law, which demonstrated that all the known chemical elements composed an integrated system.

The *zemstvo* reform of 1864 introduced new vitality into provincial life by providing a genuine, if limited, sphere of public activity. *Zemstvos* were elected institutions of local self-government in which men from all sectors of society, including newly freed peasants, held the right to participate. Responsible for looking after rural economic and cultural needs, they built and staffed hospitals and dispensaries that offered peasants a kind of socialized medicine. The schools that *zemstvos* established furthered popular education, with modest but still meaningful results. By the turn of the twentieth century, the combined efforts of *zemstvo*, state schools, and church-run parish schools had raised the rate of popular literacy to slightly under 29 percent of rural people aged nine to forty-nine. *Zemstvos* also expanded job opportunities for members of the educated middle classes—as teachers, statisticians, agronomists, physicians, medical assistants, and the like.

The judicial reform of 1864, which established a basis for the rule of law, was the most far-reaching. For the first time, it required professional training for judges and granted them secure tenure, which brought relative independence from outside pressure, including pressure from the state. With trials open to the public, juries that decided criminal cases, and lawyers who engaged in adversarial procedures, courtrooms became a sphere of relatively free speech. In 1874, the army was transformed as well. Men of all social backgrounds, conscripted for six years of active service and nine more in the reserves, replaced the army of conscript peasants who had faced twenty-five years of service. The tsar, however, rejected appeals to establish an elected, representative body with a voice in government affairs. Autocracy remained intact and the power of the ruler, absolute. Most historians agree that these shortcomings limited the overall effectiveness of the Great Reforms. They nevertheless introduced the most far-reaching changes since the reign of Peter the Great and their impact was extensive and long lasting.

To a vocal minority of people anticipating more fundamental transformation, however, they seemed too little, too late. University students, more humbly born than those of earlier generations and less respectful of social proprieties, were particularly prominent among these radicals. Their contemporaries entitled them "nihilists." They adopted the term from Ivan Turgenev's novel, *Fathers and Children* (1862), which dramatized the tensions between liberal Westernizers of an earlier generation and the rebellious young. Following the emancipation, small groups began calling for a revolution to give peasants all the land and end Russia's autocratic order. In 1866, the former student Dmitrii Karakozov, acting alone, attempted unsuccessfully to assassinate the tsar. His example inspired Sergei Nechaev, son of a former serf and a student leader, a man dedicated to revolution by any means necessary. In 1869 Nechaev convinced members of his small, conspiratorial organization to murder a member he suspected of disloyalty. The body was soon discovered and scores of radicals arrested. The political unrest of the decade, widely reported in the contemporary press, inspired Feodor Dostoevsky to write *The Demons* (1872). It depicted a world in upheaval, where violence erupts and ideologies collide.

A new and far larger radical movement quickly replaced the arrested conspirators. Its members, drawn from a new, younger generation, now included a substantial minority of women. Many of them were students at higher education courses for women—not quite universities—that began to open at the end of the 1860s in Moscow and St. Petersburg. Repelled by Nechaev's ruthless methods, participants in this new movement were committed to adopting only moral means to reach their goal: a peasant-based, social revolution. They became known as populists (*narodniki*). Like Aleksandr Herzen, populists believed that peasants were inherently socialist by virtue of their egalitarian, communal self-government and ownership of land. A peasant revolution would thus enable Russia to achieve an agrarian form of socialism while bypassing capitalism, which Russian radicals rejected as a source of suffering and economic injustice. By contrast, Karl Marx and Friedrich Engels, whose writings increasingly influenced European socialist movements, regarded capitalism as a necessary stage en route to the socialist future.

Like many members of the movement, the nobly born Vera Figner, who abandoned her medical studies in Zurich, Switzerland, to become a full-time revolutionary, believed in the imminence of revolution: "The people would rise up (and we were sure that at this point the army would desert to their side) and proclaim the abolition of private property and inheritance rights." Socialism would quickly follow. "The land, the factories and the mills would be declared public property. After the social revolution, everyone would have to perform physical labor. Their needs would be satisfied by the product of their labor—which would be at the disposal of society as a whole. Society would also care for the sick, the elderly, and the crippled."[3]

In the summer of 1872, eighteen-year-old Sofia Perovskaya, daughter of a former governor of St. Petersburg and a former student at the Alarchinsky courses for women, left for the countryside, having learned to give vaccinations from a *zemstvo* physician. Like thousands of others who went "to the people" in this period, she hoped to gain the trust of the peasantry and incline them to revolution. Walking from village to village, sleeping and eating in peasant huts, she dispensed socialist propaganda in addition to vaccinating peasant children. Despite these efforts, neither she nor other populists managed to spark a popular uprising. Instead, making easy targets for the police, they were harassed, questioned, or imprisoned by the thousands.

In frustration, some turned to violence. The example of Vera Zasulich, a young noblewoman, emboldened them. In January 1878, Zasulich shot the municipal governor of St. Petersburg to avenge his mistreatment of a political prisoner. Tried as a criminal in the newly created court system, she was acquitted by a jury. Western European leftists as well as much of Russia's educated public celebrated Zasulich as a heroine. After her acquittal, radical violence escalated, splitting the populist movement. One faction, proponents of terror calling themselves the People's Will, launched a campaign to assassinate the tsar that was widely reported abroad. On March 1, 1881, the small group of committed revolutionaries succeeded. They then paid with their lives for the victory in their duel with the autocratic state. Sofia Perovskaya, who orchestrated the assassination after the arrest of Andrei Zhelyabov, was hanged along with him and three other men, the first woman in Russian history to be executed for a political crime.

Their act brought unintended political consequences. Terrorists failed to achieve either widespread popular uprisings or the concessions they sought—above all, a constitution and civil liberties. Rather, waves of arrests crushed the revolutionary movement. The new ruler, Tsar Alexander III, proved far more conservative than his father. He was greatly influenced by Konstantin Pobedonostsev, the procurator general of the Holy Synod, the governing body of the church. Suspicious of any form of popular sovereignty, Pobedonostsev believed that ordinary people were incapable of ruling themselves: "In the democratic form of government, the real rulers are the dexterous manipulators of votes, with their placemen, the mechanics who so skillfully operate the hidden springs, which move the puppets in the arena of democratic elections. Men of this kind are ever ready with loud speeches lauding equality; in reality, they rule the people as any despot or military dictator might rule it."[4]

The tsar reaffirmed autocracy as the best form of rule for Russia's peoples and rejected Western influences as antithetical to the Russian national spirit. Alexander III also sought to curtail his father's reforms, convinced that they had moved the empire in the wrong direction. Political trials were transferred from civil to military courts, circumventing the new legal protections. The police and local officials gained extraordinary repressive power; the authority of the *zemstvo* was curtailed. Censorship tightened. As embodied by Tsar Alexander III, Holy Orthodox Russia, an idealized version of the past before Peter the Great's innovations, became celebrated as never before. The ruler's death in 1894 and the ascension of his son, Nicholas II, changed little. This was a grim period for critical intellectuals, conveyed in the short stories of Anton Chekhov, whose melancholy characters nurture doomed hopes and dreams.

Presenting the empire as Orthodox and Russian altered the previous policy of tolerance toward non-Russian subjects. Peoples in the western borderlands felt the shift most acutely. The seeds had been sown decades before, in formerly Polish regions under Russian rule. In January 1863, Poles murdered Russian soldiers sleeping in their barracks during a short-lived revolt against Russian dominion. The uprising aroused public sentiment against the Poles and inspired official efforts to prevent further challenges to imperial unity. The *zemstvo* and judicial reforms, which encouraged local initiative, were not implemented in areas inhabited by Poles, Lithuanians, Belorussians, and Jews. Instead, the regime endeavored to assimilate these groups, with the ultimate goal of cultural uniformity—that is, of making them "Russian." This policy of cultural Russification brought new insistence on the use of the Russian language in administration and schools in Poland, Ukraine, and Belarus. After 1881, the celebration of Russian distinctiveness and superiority intensified these Russifying trends, and they were introduced into other parts of the empire, such as the Baltic provinces and, in the early twentieth century, Finland.

Russia's Jews suffered acutely from the change. Following the assassination of Alexander II, violent attacks against Jews erupted in scores of cities, for reasons that remain in dispute among historians. They were called pogroms (from the Russian verb, *pogromit'*, to destroy with violence), a word that has entered the global lexicon. Alexander III was openly anti-Semitic, as were many of those around him. "In the depth of my heart, I am always happy when they beat the Jews, but still we must not allow it," he once remarked to the governor general of Warsaw.[5] Believing that by their behavior Jews brought popular violence upon themselves, his government banned new Jewish settlements in rural areas even in the Pale of Settlement and introduced quotas for Jews in high schools, institutions of higher education, and the professions of medicine and law, in which the proportion of Jews had grown dramatically since the 1860s. Jewish integration into the larger society slowed. Millions of Jews left Russia over the following decades. The majority headed for the United States, but a growing minority settled in Ottoman Palestine, which Zionists viewed as their homeland.

The new nationalist vision also shaped the economic policy pursued by Russia's ministers of finance, in particular Sergei Witte, appointed to the post in 1892. Born in Tbilisi (now the capital of Georgia) and educated in the cosmopolitan Black Sea port of Odessa, Witte was the son of a Baltic German father and Russian mother. While very much a product of Russia's multiethnic empire, Witte embraced the tsar's Russo-centric vision. To achieve the industrial development necessary to ensure Russia's self-defense and global competitiveness, he further increased the state's already powerful role in the economy. Subsidizing railroads and key industries, establishing tariffs to protect them, the state obtained the requisite capital by borrowing heavily abroad and squeezing taxes from the rural population.

Witte also strove to attract private foreign investment, confident that Russia would be strong enough to resist foreign influence. Attracting investment became easier after 1897, when Russia adopted the gold standard, and the ruble became convertible to other currencies. By the outbreak of World War I, foreign capital comprised as much as half of the investments in new Russian industries. Certain sectors of the economy were almost wholly foreign owned: metallurgy, the Ukrainian coalfields, and the oil fields of Baku. In those oil fields—located on the western shore of the Caspian Sea, which had been acquired from Persia in 1813—the Swedish-born Nobel brothers introduced pumps and pipelines then in use in the United States to replace primitive methods of extraction and transport, vastly increasing both production and profitability. In 1901, the brothers established the Nobel Prizes with part of their profits. Russia's share of the global economy increased markedly. Between 1870 and 1900, its contribution to world steel production grew from 2 percent to 8 percent. Until it was overtaken by the United States in the first quarter of the twentieth century, Russia became the world's leading extractor of oil.

Railroads powered economic growth. From about 850 miles in 1855, railroad track expanded to about 40,000 miles by 1905. Employing close to half a million people, more than any other non-agricultural sector of the economy, railroads stimulated development in other sectors, heavy industry in particular. Sergei Witte was convinced that railroads also held the key to Russia's imperial ambitions in the east. He enticed the tsar with a vision of the longest railroad in the world, some 4,500 miles in length. Running from Moscow to Russia's

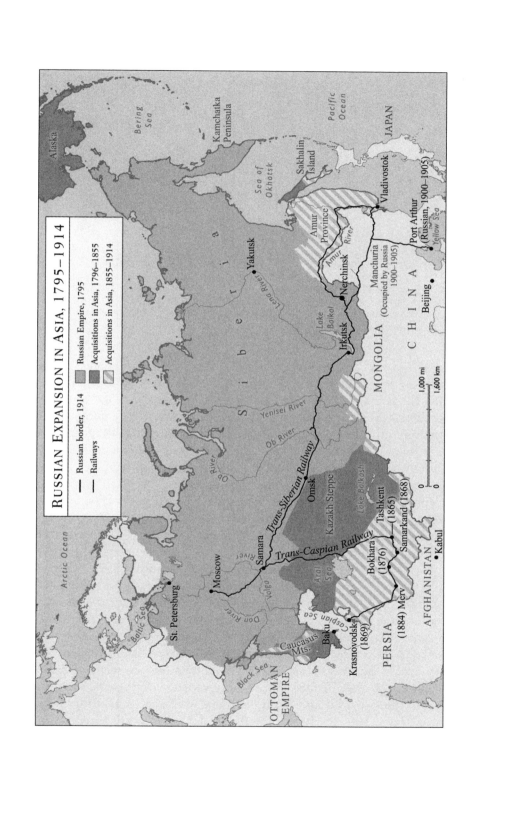

RUSSIAN EXPANSION IN ASIA, 1795–1914

— Russian border, 1914
— Railways

Russian Empire, 1795
Acquisitions in Asia, 1796–1855
Acquisitions in Asia, 1855–1914

A group of peasant migrants travel to Siberia on the Trans-Siberian Railroad, visible behind them. After the railroad's completion in 1891, peasant migration to the east grew rapidly, as peasants left overcrowded villages in search of a better livelihood. Library of Congress, LCUSZ6-1782.

Pacific port of Vladivostok, it would further the integration of Siberia into the empire and the exploitation of Siberia's rich natural resources. The railroad would also facilitate Russia's penetration of Asia, where the United States, Japan, Britain, France, and Germany competed for economic advantage in a newly vulnerable China. Pulling ahead of these rivals, Witte won Chinese agreement for the construction of a shortcut to Vladivostok through Chinese Northern Manchuria. Two years later, in 1898, the Chinese agreed to allow Russia to lease an ice-free port on the Pacific, Port Arthur, and to build a railroad spur to this new "window on the East." The penetration of Manchuria marked the beginning of Russian conquest. It would eventuate, in 1904, in a fateful war with Japan

Drawing together the vast expanses of the empire, the railroad held the potential to transform the economies and ways of life not only of Russians but also of native peoples, barely touched by the policy of Russification, which affected primarily the western borderlands. The railroad offered relief to peasants in the heartland. Their numbers had doubled between the emancipation and the turn of the century, with no comparable increase in land. With government encouragement, tens of thousands of peasants abandoned impoverished and overcrowded villages to travel by rail and resettle in the east. Most headed for Siberia, where Slavs came vastly to outnumber natives. Conflicts with native peoples over land intensified. On the Kazakh steppes south of the

In the 1880s, Koranic schools such as this one comprised part of the movement to improve the position of Muslims in the Russian empire by liberating Islam from Western domination. The schools introduced new methods of studying Arabic, and in the higher classes, taught modern sciences and languages.
Library of Congress, Proskudin-Gorskii Collection, LC-DIG-prok-02304.

Trans-Siberian line, Slavic settlers seized the best pasturelands, driving nomads farther south to graze their herds.

Railroads facilitated the partial economic integration of Central Asia, the last redoubt of the former Mongol empire. Ever since the Civil War in the United States had severed supplies of cotton, owners of textile factories in Russia had pressed for more aggressive policies in the region, which boasted conditions suitable for cotton growing. They welcomed the conquest of Central Asia, completed by the early 1880s and the construction of a railway line linking the Caspian Sea to Samarkand, and subsequently, the cities of Tashkent and Andijan. Replacing transport by camelback over endless miles of desert, the Trans-Caspian railroad made Central Asian cotton competitive with cotton from foreign sources.

When Nikolai Varentsov visited in the early 1890s on behalf of his Moscow trading firm, he traveled by boat from Baku over a stormy Caspian and then, more comfortably, by rail. In Samarkand and Tashkent, local merchants seeking to expand their already flourishing cotton trade, Jewish as well as Muslim, entertained Varentsov with lavish hospitality. By 1910, cotton production occupied almost 20 percent of Central Asia's arable land, about half of that in the Ferghana valley. It became a kind of economic colony of Russia.

At least in the short run, however, Russia's economic development and integration into the global economy worsened rural poverty, much as globalization does in developing countries today. Squeezed hard by taxation, forced by tariff policy to pay high prices for consumer goods, peasants also received far less than usual for their harvests. This was a result of the mid-century revolution in transport, which inundated world markets with grain. Steamers carried New World crops to European shores; railroads conveyed them inland. By the mid-1890s, world grain prices had dropped to half of what they were twenty years earlier. Peasants fell ever further behind in their tax and redemption payments. In 1891, famine struck some of Russia's most fertile regions, and hunger or hunger-related disease stole the lives of hundreds of thousands. In 1901 and 1902, famine struck again. Peasants looked to more land as the solution to their poverty. With money borrowed from state or private banks, enterprising peasants bought land from nobles, many of whom were also unable to cope with new market conditions. By 1905, noble landowners had lost over 40 percent of their post-emancipation holdings. Peasants coveted the rest, convinced that land they had tilled in the days of serfdom remained rightfully theirs.

Even as it fostered misery, economic development also encouraged unprecedented geographic and social mobility. Millions of peasants, women as well as men, left their villages to take advantage of new employment opportunities. They streamed into Russia's cities, especially Moscow and St. Petersburg. In both, peasants—identified as such by the internal passports they were required to carry—far outnumbered all other social groups by the close of the nineteenth century. Some, like the sixteen-year-old peasant Semeon Kanatchikov, left for the city eagerly: "I wanted to rid myself of the monotony of village life as quickly as possible, to free myself from my father's despotism and tutelage, to begin to live a self-reliant, independent life," he remembered of his departure for Moscow.[6]

But others, such as Olga and Pavel Mitrofanov, went elsewhere because they could no longer make a living in their village. Like many unskilled migrants, Pavel had to take whatever job he could find. He worked as a watchman in one part of Moscow; in another, Olga worked as a domestic servant, the most common job for migrant women. The couple saw one another only on their day off. Low wages combined with the high cost of urban housing made family life almost impossible for most migrants. Most male workers left their wives and children in the village, visiting from time to time. Virtually bereft of adult men, some villages in the vicinity of Moscow and St. Petersburg became known as "women's kingdoms."

Living and working away from home might change a peasant migrant. Skilled workers like Semeon Kanatchikov, who underwent a lengthy apprenticeship before he became a metalworker, often acquired a new identity. They exchanged their homespun clothing for fashionable and factory-made garb, and experienced a heightened sense of dignity. But even factory workers lacking skills gained a sense of collective strength from their growing numbers and common plight. They became less tolerant of demeaning treatment by foremen and managers, of starvation wages, of laboring for fourteen or more hours a day, six days a week. Despite laws that forbade strikes and unions, thousands of factory workers periodically went out on strike demanding improvement in their conditions. In 1897, they won legislation limiting the workday to eleven and one half hours in large enterprises. In study circles held after working hours, radical intellectuals sought to awaken workers to their economic and political oppression. Kanatchikov became drawn to the ideas of Karl Marx; so did others like him.

Marx, whose ideas would shape Russian developments for almost three-quarters of a century, regarded capitalism as a necessary stage of historical development. He predicted that capitalism, while exploiting and creating misery for workers, would forge a global economy and usher in material abundance capable of satisfying the needs of all. Under capitalism, however, only the owners of capital would benefit. Almost everyone else would be reduced to the level of proletarians—that is, workers who had nothing to sell but their labor power. Marxism attracted workers because it explained their suffering and made them the motor of decisive historical change: their revolution would usher in a higher stage of historical development, an era of economic justice known as socialism.

Rapid economic change drew different responses from Russia's burgeoning middle classes. Russians who were engaged in commerce, prime beneficiaries of policies promoting economic growth, tended to be loyal to the throne and to be economic as well as cultural nationalists. Embracing their Slavic heritage, they lavished their new wealth on philanthropy and on distinctively Russian art and music. The textile magnate Pavel Tretyakov, for example, assembled an enormous collection of Russian realist masterpieces. Bequeathed to the city of Moscow in 1892, it is still displayed in the gallery that bears his name. In his private opera house, the Moscow railroad magnate Savva Mamontov promoted the compositions of Modest Mussorgsky and Nikolai Rimsky-Korsakov, which drew on Russian history and folklore in pursuit of a native musical tradition. The impresario Sergei Dyaghilev exported Russian culture to Paris. His Ballets Russes, which featured the work of Russia's modernist artists and composers, soon put Russia in the forefront of the international avant-garde. As they became available in translation, the groundbreaking psychological novels of Feodor Dostoevsky had much the same impact on Russia's literary stature, despite the author's hostility to Western individualism and capitalism, and to liberalism as well as socialism.

But other members of the middle classes grew more critical of the autocratic government and its economic policies. For them, the famine of 1891 was a turning point. Widely reported in the press, it awakened educated people to popular misery, which many blamed on the government's economic policies. Liberal professionals became more restive. Resenting their exclusion from political life and helpless to better the lives of Russia's suffering masses, Russia's liberals aspired to a constitutional order and representative form of government. The Russian Social Democratic Labor Party (RSDLP) formed in 1898, uniting various Marxist groups. In 1901, populism reemerged in the form of the Socialist Revolutionary Party, which now embraced factory workers as well as peasants in its vision of social revolution. Both attracted university students, the most radical in Europe. Like its populist forerunner, the Socialist Revolutionary Party embraced terror as a tactic of struggle. In 1902, a Socialist Revolutionary assassinated Dmitrii Sipyagin, repressive minister of the interior, and in 1904, his successor Vyacheslav von Plehve.

All elements of the opposition became inflamed by Russia's performance in the war with Japan, which broke out over control of Manchuria. On January 27, 1904, the Japanese, intending to reverse Russian expansion into the region, launched a surprise attack on Port Arthur, where the Russians had based a naval fleet. In the war that followed, Russia suffered defeat after defeat instead of attaining what it anticipated to be an easy victory. Its armaments proved technically inferior to the weaponry of the Japanese, its ossified military command no match for theirs. In May 1905, the Japanese destroyed Russia's entire Baltic fleet, which had sailed halfway around the world to engage the Japanese in the straits of Tushima.

Military failures lowered the prestige of the autocracy and emboldened the liberation movement, as the opposition came to be called. Even forward thinking members of the landowning nobility, ordinarily a conservative group, began to sympathize with the goal of constitutional change. Workers in growing numbers went out on strike. Political terror escalated. Then, a peaceful march of workers and their families to petition the ruler provided the spark that ignited a revolution. The workers' petition began in the usual way, supplicating the tsar and pleading for his mercy:

> Sovereign!
> We, workers and inhabitants of the city of St. Petersburg, members of various estates of the realm, our wives, children, and helpless old parents, have come to you, Sovereign, to seek justice and protection. We are impoverished and oppressed, we are burdened with work, and insulted. We are treated not like humans [but] like slaves who must suffer a bitter fate and keep silent.... We have come to that terrible moment when it is better to die than to continue unbearable sufferings.

But, having begun so humbly, the petition went on to request far-reaching changes, including complete civil liberties, a constituent assembly, universal suffrage and a secret ballot, and equality of all before the law, as well as the eight-hour workday and other "measures against the oppression of labor by capital."[7] Tsarist troops opened fire on the marchers, killing at least one hundred and wounding scores more. The event, which occurred on January 9, 1905, became known as "Bloody Sunday."

In the upheaval that ensued, it seemed as if all of Russia had united in opposition to the ruling order. Industrial workers, students, professionals, even nobles and industrialists became caught up in the wave of resistance that swept over the country. They formed unions, still forbidden, to demand their rights. Not only workers, but also professionals, women, Jews, and in July 1905, peasants joined the union movement. Emboldened by the evident weakness of the state, peasants rose up in rebellion. Acting collectively to satisfy their hunger for land, they attacked the estates of noble landowners, often their former owners,

With soldiers standing by in the foreground, their bayonets aloft, a gigantic skeleton representing official repression tramples demonstrating workers in December 1905 in Moscow, knocking over barricades and crushing the people on the streets. An outcry against the violent suppression of the revolution of 1905, this cartoon, which appeared in a new satirical journal, is also evidence of the greatly expanded freedom of the press. Boris Kustodiev, "Invasion," *Zhupei*, no. 2, 1905. The Slavic and Baltic Division, New York Public Library, Astor, Lenox and Tilden Foundations.

aiming to drive them away. Unrest spread beyond the Russian heartland and into the Baltic Provinces, Ukraine, Poland, and the Caucasus. In June, sailors on the battleship *Potemkin*, anchored in Odessa, mutinied. So did some troops returning from the war with Japan. It had ended in late August 1905 with the Treaty of Portsmouth, mediated by President Theodore Roosevelt of the United States.

The revolution peaked in October 1905. A widely supported general strike—even factory owners, normally conservative, endorsed it—brought business to a halt and the empire to its knees. On October 17, Nicholas II finally capitulated. His October Manifesto, which promised civil and political liberties and an elected representative body, the Duma, seemed to transform Russia into a constitutional monarchy. Liberals celebrated it as a victory. Socialists, including radical workers who sought an end to monarchy and a democratic republic, were dissatisfied with the Manifesto and continued to resist, but ineffectually without liberal support. The manifesto also failed to satisfy peasants, whose chief desire was land. Peasant unrest intensified in 1906. Nevertheless, destroying the unity that empowered the revolution, the tsar's concession brought it to a close.

CHAPTER 7

Wars and Revolutions
(1905–1945)

On November 1, 1916, just about a decade after the Duma, promised by Nicholas II in his October Manifesto, first went into session, Pavel Milyukov took the floor to denounce his government's disastrous conduct in the Great War then raging in Europe. Enumerating failure after failure on the battlefield and at home, Milyukov repeatedly inquired: "Is this stupidity, or is this treason?"[1] A professor of history and head of Russia's foremost liberal party, Milyukov, in an outburst of patriotism, had put aside his pacifism and oppositional politics at the onset of war with Germany and the Austro-Hungarian Empire to support the tsarist government. Milyukov's speech transformed him into a popular hero. Four months later, popular unrest brought down the tsarist regime. The liberal-led coalition that replaced it, initially shaped by Milyukov himself, lasted a mere eight months before the Bolshevik Party, a Marxist organization, overthrew it and began efforts to construct the world's first socialist society.

The Bolshevik Party's leader, Vladimir Lenin, had opposed the war from the first, unlike most socialists in Russia and abroad. Convinced that the war was fought over imperialist spoils, Lenin urged workers to turn their guns on their own capitalists instead of their brother worker-soldiers on the battlefields, and transform an imperialist war into a socialist revolution. "Working men of the world, unite!" Karl Marx and Friedrich Engels had urged at the conclusion of their *Communist Manifesto*. Embracing this view, Lenin's revolutionary state rejected the nationalism and liberal politics espoused not only by men such as Milyukov, but also by Russia's wartime allies—Great Britain, France, and the United States—in favor of revolutionary internationalism. The state that Lenin would build heralded a more general European shift toward dictatorial rule in the interwar period. It would also offer a vision of the good life, based on socialist principles, that profoundly challenged Western capitalism and individualism.

Historians continue to debate whether Tsar Nicholas II would have retained power had war not intervened. By 1914, a mixture of harsh repression and limited concession had restored a measure of social peace after the 1905 revolution. Repression was particularly brutal in peasant villages and the borderlands, where nationalist unrest had challenged the empire's unity. On the periphery of its empire, the regime supplemented repression with efforts to divide and rule. In the Baltic provinces, it set the privileged Germans against Latvians and Estonians; in the Transcaucasus, Christian Armenians against Muslims. Everywhere, it set Russian loyalists against Jews, whom emergent right-wing movements blamed for the unrest in 1905. While the authorities stood aside, in the fall of 1905 anti-Semitic pogroms murdered about a thousand Jews. But even as unrest subsided and avant-garde culture flourished as never before, new grievances joined older ones. The Duma lacked genuine power and proved mainly a debating society, prompting liberals like Milyukov to despair of further reform. The regime soon curtailed workers' newly won right to organize. Their working and living conditions as bad as before, more than a million workers walked out on strike in the six months preceding the outbreak of World War I. At that point a burst of patriotism, which temporarily united society and eased pre-war tensions, brought worker unrest to a halt.

World War I, the first "total war," destroyed the fragile domestic peace. Aerial bombardment, and the mass deployment of the machine guns, artillery pieces and tanks used in this war, transformed killing from a face-to-face to a mechanized process, for which modern industrial production proved crucial. The war dragged on for four years, took the lives of more than nine million soldiers, and wounded many more. Everywhere in Europe, it placed unprecedented demands on economies, peoples, and governments. Men of military age disappeared into the maw of combat. Industries geared for military production. Civilians suffered as food and consumer goods grew scarce. To maintain national unity amid these pressures, governments vastly expanded their reach. They controlled the news, quashed dissent, and regulated labor, supplies, and prices. The demands of warfare eventually destroyed every contiguous pre-war European empire, the Austro-Hungarian, German, and Ottoman as well Russian.

Russia's was the first to fall. Although its army was the largest in the war, it was poorly led, equipped, and trained, and was easily outmatched by the German army. Each defeat lowered morale on the home front. Hardship undermined morale still further. With almost all resources headed for the front, food and other prime necessities grew scarce and expensive. Labor conditions deteriorated; bread lines lengthened; inflation skyrocketed. The divide between rich and poor deepened. In December 1915, a policeman in Petrograd (the new, patriotic name for St. Petersburg) observed rising social tensions: "All these women, freezing in twenty-degree weather for hours on end in order to receive two pounds of sugar or two to three pounds of flour, understandably look for the person responsible for their woes." They partly blamed wealthy ladies, who could buy even expensive goods immediately, thus contributing to scarcity.[2]

Strikes resumed a year after the war began. In addition to better working conditions, strikers demanded an end to war and political change. Ethnic tensions tore at the fabric of empire. The army command, its Russian nationalism exacerbated by war, forcibly deported Germans and foreigners and at least a million Jews from the western borderlands, labeling them "enemy subjects." Inundating the internal provinces, deportees further strained local resources and earned the ire of local people. In Central Asia, Kirghiz men, hitherto exempt from the draft, violently resisted efforts to conscript them.

Tsar Nicholas II made the situation worse by insisting on his autocratic prerogatives. He felt threatened by the civic organizations that addressed some of the demands of total war and resisted liberal efforts to form a government that might unify the nation and gain popular support for the war. Then, to the horror of his advisors, in August 1915 he departed for the front, having declared himself commander-in-chief of the army. He left the controls to his wife, Alexandra, popularly known as the "German" empress because of her German birth, although in fact by upbringing she was more English than German. Rumor had it that she took her orders from Grigorii Rasputin, a purported holy man infamous for his sexual excesses but able to cure the hemophiliac attacks of Alexis, the heir to the throne. Competent ministers lost their positions; incompetent reactionaries replaced them. Groundless but widespread rumors of a sexual liaison between Rasputin and Alexandra further undermined respect for the throne. Hoping to save the regime from itself, in December 1916 several monarchists murdered Rasputin.

Revolution began two months later, on February 23, 1917 (according to the Russian calendar; March 8, by the Western; International Women's Day by both), when thousands of housewives and women workers poured into the streets to protest the food situation. Over the following days, hundreds of thousands of factory workers walked out on strike. Demands grew more radical: No more war! Down with autocracy! Ordered to suppress the rebellion, soldiers of the Petrograd garrison refused, and on February 27 they went over to the rebels' side. Their defection transformed rebellion into revolution. At the urging of his generals, Nicholas II abdicated on March 2. That same day, a liberal-led Provisional Government, its very name signifying its temporary nature, assumed formal authority until a democratically elected Constituent Assembly could be convened.

Russia's wartime allies immediately recognized the Provisional Government as the new authority. Fighting to make the world safe for democracy, as US president Woodrow Wilson put it, they were relieved to see like-minded men replace their autocratic ally. Support for the new government was more tepid at home. From the first, the Provisional Government vied for popular support with the Petrograd Soviet (meaning council) of Workers and Soldiers Deputies, which emerged at the same time, led by a coalition of socialist parties. The resulting arrangement became known as "dual power." Of the two, the Petrograd Soviet was the more powerful, because the workers and soldiers who made the revolution elected its delegates, but they had no say in the composition of the Provisional Government. The dual power arrangement quickly spread to other cities and towns, the telegraph conveying the news from Petrograd.

The end of autocracy brought complete civil liberties; the abolition of all social, religious, and national restrictions; and, after a massive demonstration in July, the inclusion of women in the newly won universal suffrage. In addition, the Petrograd Soviet, acting alone, almost completely democratized the army. Order no. 1, issued on March 1, abolished the pre-revolutionary military hierarchy, and, calling for the election of soldiers' committees in all military units, put the committees in control of weaponry. Soldiers learned about it virtually overnight and implemented it everywhere.

Over the next eight months, popular support for the Provisional Government steadily evaporated, while support for a government of soviets grew. Peasants became more radical as the Provisional Government failed to satisfy their demands for more land. Taking matters into their own hands, using threats or exercising force, they drove off nobles, seized their land and redistributed it among themselves. Another source of popular disaffection was the continuing war effort, which the Provisional Government regarded as a matter of national honor. Rank-and-file soldiers disagreed. Freed from the rigid discipline of tsarist times, most were in no mood to advance. When the

"Long Live the International Workers' Holiday, Long Live Socialism," proclaims the large banner at this demonstration held on May 1, the international socialist holiday, in 1917. *The demonstrators crowd Palace Square, to which tsarist soldiers blocked access twelve years earlier on the day that became known as Bloody Sunday. Enjoying their recently expanded rights, workers press for further concessions.* Library of Congress, LC-USZ62-25295.

Provisional Government ordered an attack against German forces on the Galician front in mid-June 1917, it soon turned into a rout. Units mutinied, refusing to follow orders, and desertion rates skyrocketed. As Lenin put it, soldiers voted for peace with their feet. Furthermore, the Provisional Government proved no more able than the tsarist regime to resolve the economic problems that led to unrest in February. Over the summer, the situation deteriorated: inflation eroded wage gains, bread lines lengthened, and violent crime escalated. Russia's many ethnic minorities also grew alienated, their demands for greater autonomy within the empire ignored by the Provisional Government. By the fall of 1917, few Russians were prepared to risk their lives on the government's behalf.

This was the moment Lenin had long been waiting for. Born Vladimir Ulyanov (Lenin was a revolutionary pseudonym) in Simbirsk, located along the Volga River east of Moscow, he came from a background that reflected Russia's complex ethnic and social heritage. His mother was of Swedish-German extraction, and his father, a serf's son who earned noble status as a school inspector, was of Kalmyk and German, Ukrainian, or Jewish origin—this detail remains contested. Expelled in 1887 from Kazan University for participating in student disorders, Lenin devoted himself to socialist revolution and forged a political party, eventually named the Bolsheviks, that reflected his views. A theorist as well as an activist, he adapted the ideas of Karl Marx to the Russian setting. Marx had envisioned a workers' revolution occurring in advanced capitalist states, where mass production would satisfy human needs and worker-proletarians would predominate. Russia was still an agricultural society, and capitalism was just beginning. Unwilling to abandon the goal of revolution, Lenin emphasized the leading role of a party like the Bolsheviks, the increasing impoverishment of Russia's peasantry, and Russia's position as the weakest link in a world capitalist system. If socialist revolution succeeded in Russia, he believed, worker risings all over Europe and eventually, throughout the world, would follow. Thereafter, proletarian internationalism—the brotherhood of workers premised by Marx—would replace "bourgeois" (that is, middle class) nationalism, rendering war unnecessary. Society, not capitalists, would own the means of production, ending exploitation, bringing economic equality, and enabling workers to reap the full fruits of their labor.

At Lenin's urging, on October 25–26, 1917, the Bolsheviks, acting alone and without the support of other socialist parties represented in the soviets, overthrew the Provisional Government in the name of a government of soviets. Declared Lenin:

> Comrades, the workmen's and peasants' revolution, the need of which the Bolsheviks have emphasized many times, has come to pass.
>
> What is the significance of this revolution? In the first place, that we shall have a soviet government, without the participation of the bourgeoisie of any kind. The oppressed masses will of themselves form a government.... One of our immediate tasks is to put an end to war at once. But in order to end the war, which is closely bound up with the present capitalist system, it is necessary to overthrow capitalism itself. In this work we shall have the aid of the world labor movement.[3]

Despite the establishment of a government of soviets, the Bolshevik Party retained the real power. Over the following months, it assumed control of Moscow and other cities, sometimes non-violently, sometimes, as in Moscow, only after considerable bloodshed.

Lenin and his followers immediately set about implementing their vision of a workers' state. All land was transferred to those who

Speaking from a podium, Vladimir Lenin points toward the future and the imminent triumph of socialism. "A specter is haunting Europe, the specter of communism" reads the caption beneath him, quoting the opening lines of The Communist Manifesto *by Karl Marx and Friedrich Engels.* Courtesy of the Russian and Soviet Poster Collection, Hoover Institution Archives, Stanford, California.

tilled it, validating peasant seizures. National groups were granted the right to self-determination, at least on paper. The separation of church and state, introduced under the Provisional Government, became more thoroughgoing, and religious instruction was forbidden in schools. Factory workers gained the eight-hour day, the right to supervise production, and a new privileged status. The "bourgeoisie"—that is, those who had formerly enjoyed wealth and privilege—suffered the expropriation of their property and a range of legal and financial penalties. New laws granted women complete equality with men. Marriage was removed from the authority of the church; divorce, once difficult and expensive, became easily accessible. Children born to unmarried couples acquired full legal rights. Working women were entitled to eight weeks of paid maternity leave, before or after childbirth. In 1920, abortion became legal if performed by a physician. Co-education became the rule.

In January 1918, the Russian calendar became identical to that in use elsewhere.

Soon after the Bolsheviks seized power, Pavel Milyukov headed south. His destination was the Don region, where General Mikhail Alekseev, de facto commander of Russia's armies since 1915, was organizing armed resistance. The Bolsheviks' coup d'état enjoyed support from a substantial portion of the working class and a smaller sector of the peasantry. However, it alienated just about everyone else. Opposition grew in size and diversity after their regime dispersed the democratically elected Constituent Assembly in January 1918, and then, after German troops threatened to invade Petrograd, forcing the Bolsheviks to abandon it for Moscow, concluded the draconian Treaty of Brest-Litovsk in March. The Treaty deprived Russia of the Western regions of its former empire and part of Transcaucasia. By late spring 1918, Russia was engulfed in a brutal civil war that would take the lives of millions. The Bolshevik Reds fought the Whites—monarchists, liberals, moderate socialists, peasants seeking freedom from the state, and non-Russians. Pursuing different goals, these varied White groups never succeeded in joining forces.

White leaders were sometimes aided and abetted by foreign powers. These included Japan, Great Britain, France, and the United States, which regarded the Bolshevik regime as subversives. In Siberia, where Admiral Kolchak led White forces, British assistance was crucial: "Since about the middle of December [1918] every round of rifle ammunition fired on the front has been of British manufacture, conveyed to Vladivostok in British ships and delivered at Omsk by British Guards," reported General Alfred Knox, chief British officer in Siberia, in June 1919.[4] Russia's former allies sent troops as well as material assistance, and in the north, they fought alongside Whites. The intervention was never sufficient to ensure a White victory, however. It only confirmed Bolshevik beliefs about capitalist hostility to their revolutionary workers' state. The Red Army maintained control of the heartland, always outnumbered White forces, and proved far better able to earn the loyalty of peasant conscripts. By 1920, the triumphant Red Army could begin mopping up pockets of peasant and national resistance. It marched into Georgia, birthplace of the future dictator, Joseph Stalin, and, driving out its moderate socialist leadership, ended Georgia's brief independence. Rebels in Central Asia whom the regime labeled *basmachis* (bandits) resisted longer, even after the summer of 1922, when the regime formally subdued the region.

Red victory in the civil war came at an enormous cost. Both Reds and Whites used terror against perceived enemies. The years of violence transformed the Bolsheviks—who renamed themselves communists in 1918—and the society they ruled. War exacerbated the party's authoritarian tendencies and accustomed its members to suspect enemies everywhere and solve problems at gunpoint. In December 1917 the regime created the Cheka, a secret police organization, to crush threats to the revolution. Its numbers expanded dramatically during the civil war years. Enjoying virtually unlimited power to arrest and execute suspected counterrevolutionaries, the Cheka became a law unto itself. It was the forerunner of all subsequent secret police, including the KGB.

The tsar became one of many casualties of revolutionary violence. To prevent him from becoming a rallying point for counterrevolution, local Bolsheviks executed him and his family in mid-July 1918, as White armies approached Ekaterinburg in the Ural Mountains, where the family was being held. On September 2, the anniversary of the date French revolutionaries launched the Reign of Terror in 1793, "Red Terror" was unleashed in response to a failed attempt to assassinate Lenin and another prominent leader. Thousands were arrested or lost their lives. By 1921, the regime had silenced dissenting voices, shut opposition newspapers, and banned opposition parties.

The economy was in shambles. The years of combat wrecked much of the infrastructure. Economic policy made matters worse. Soon after seizing power, the regime nationalized banks and industrial enterprises, abolished private real estate and trade, and, in response to the escalating crisis, instituted a dictatorship over the food supply. Rationing began, on a class basis. Workers received the highest—but still inadequate—ration. To supply it, urban food detachments took grain by force from peasants unwilling to surrender it, at gunpoint if necessary. Still hungry, workers headed for their villages, emptying cities. Members of the "bourgeoisie," who were issued starvation rations or were denied them altogether, struggled to survive or fled abroad. Returning from England to Russia in 1919 to assist her imprisoned husband, the aristocratic Sofia Volkonskaya discovered to her dismay that "hostels did not exist, there were no apartments or rooms to let; all restaurants had been closed, all shops abolished. You were not allowed to buy either a piece of bread or a pair of stockings—not even a button."[5] Millions starved to death, froze, or perished of epidemic diseases. Homeless children wandered the streets, their parents dead or unable to care for them.

Confronted with mounting popular unrest as a result of these circumstances, Lenin staged a strategic retreat. In March 1921, the sailors of the Kronstadt naval base, important allies of the Bolsheviks in 1917, rebelled against Bolshevik leadership and were brutally suppressed by government troops. Soon after, the New Economic Policy (NEP) replaced forced requisitions from the peasantry with a tax in kind, permitted private trade, and restored small-scale production to private hands. The state, however, retained control of banking, large-scale industry, and foreign commerce, and Lenin's party retained control of the state. NEP nevertheless introduced a short-lived period of experimentation and diversity in culture and the arts.

Lenin's retreat came too late to prevent famine, which struck in 1921 and continued for a year, taking the lives of millions more. But for the assistance of the United States, the death rate would have been much higher. In August 1921 the semi-private American Relief Administration (ARA), headed by Herbert Hoover, began delivering food relief to famine areas in response to the regime's appeals for help. Opposed to the revolutionary state, which the United States would not recognize until 1933, ARA officials regarded food aid as a humanitarian version of war: once hunger ended, their thinking went, popular support for the Bolsheviks would evaporate.

Soviet Russia remained alone in a hostile world. By 1921, it was clear that revolution in the advanced capitalist states of the West was unlikely, at least in the near future. It is true that the Bolshevik takeover galvanized opposition movements across the globe. Tobacco workers in Cuba formed "soviets." Revolutionary student movements erupted in Beijing, China, and Cordoba, Argentina, and soon spread across Latin America. The Mexican revolution, in its most radical phase in 1917, added Marx and Lenin to its pantheon of heroes. Within months of October, Central Europe experienced a wave of political strikes and anti-war demonstrations. None, however, resulted in an enduring, soviet-style state. Although revolutionary uprisings in Germany in November 1918 forced Emperor Wilhelm II to abdicate, power passed to moderate socialists. Communist uprisings in Berlin, Bavaria, and Hungary enjoyed only brief success before their brutal suppression.

Temporarily abandoning hope of revolution in Europe, Lenin turned to the east, where anti-imperialist struggles raised the possibility of revolutionary change. In 1921, communists seized power in Mongolia, achieving an early victory. The Communist International (Comintern), created by Moscow to oversee workers' struggles abroad, quickly gained converts in many key states of the non-Western world.

At home, the regime forged an anti-imperialist empire, pointing the way to the socialist future. Thanks to Red Army successes, the Russian empire, unlike the Austro-Hungarian and Ottoman empires, remained virtually intact. Soviet Russia became the Union of Soviet Socialist Republics (USSR, or Soviet Union), on December 30, 1922. It encompassed some 80 percent of the tsar's former subjects, minus only the western borderlands: Finland, Poland, Estonia, Latvia, and Lithuania.

The USSR pledged to honor the rights of national minorities. Designed to maximize each constituent's national homogeneity, its republics and autonomous regions were encouraged to develop their own national cultures, which the regime regarded as a stage en route to proletarian internationalism. National in form, the republics and regions would be socialist in content, adhering to the aims and values of the state. The regime instituted a kind of affirmative action program for national minorities, training native supporters and promoting them into leadership positions on the local level.

At the same time, it sought to modernize "backward" regions such as Muslim Central Asia by mobilizing women as forces for change and weakening the power of the patriarchal family. To this end, laws banned traditional practices such as child marriage and polygamy. Activists encouraged women to leave home and participate in public life. Where women wore the veil, as in Uzbekistan, a major government campaign urged them to abandon it. Husbands, fathers, and brothers responded violently, taking the lives of thousands of activists and unveiled women. Abandoning the unveiling campaign, the regime continued other modernizing policies.

After his triumph in the power struggles following Lenin's death in 1924, Joseph Stalin accelerated the Soviet modernization drive. Like several of the leaders of modern Europe, notably Napoleon and Hitler, Stalin came from the periphery of Russia's empire, not the center. Born Joseph Djugashvili in 1878 in Gori, Georgia, to a shoemaker father and laundress mother, Stalin was the product of a seminary rather than university education. Many found him crude, but he possessed an ability to handle practical matters that was rare among revolutionaries. This earned him appointment to key positions in the ever-expanding party bureaucracy, which he used for his own political advantage.

Completely in control by the late 1920s, Stalin broke with the New Economic Policy. His goal: to achieve "Socialism in One Country." Under Stalin's direction, the Soviet Union would transform itself into a modern industrial economy within a few short years: "We are fifty or a hundred years behind the advanced countries. We must make good this distance in ten years. Either we do it, or they crush us," Stalin warned in February 1931.[6] Virtually everyone across the vast expanses of the Soviet Union experienced the consequences—nomadic herders of the Kazakh steppe, hunter-gatherers of Northern Siberia—as indigenous economies were transformed and aligned more closely with the priorities and needs of Moscow.

This was a revolution from above. Stalin's plans for modernizing the economy called for the collectivization of agriculture. Forced implementation of the policy, begun in the fall of 1929, was accompanied by a campaign to liquidate another enemy, *kulaks*—supposedly wealthy peasants, deemed exploiters of their less well-to-do neighbors. Confiscating the property of alleged *kulak* families and driving them from their houses, collectivization brigades terrorized the countryside. Millions of families were arrested, exiled to Siberia, Central Asia, or the far north, or forced to become laborers at new industrial sites. Their fate facilitated collectivization. When collectivizers pressured reluctant peasants to surrender their plots of land, animals, and agricultural equipment and join collective farms, or Kazakh nomads on the Central Asian steppes to take up sedentary farming, fear of being labeled a *kulak* provided a powerful incentive to agree. Nevertheless, peasants resisted, women especially, in actions the regime condemned as *bab'i bunty* (old women's riots). Peasants killed their livestock and destroyed their equipment rather than surrender them to the collective.

In non-Russian regions, resistance was fiercer still and more likely to become violent. In the Ferghana valley of Central Asia, in Chechnya in the North Caucasus, in Azerbaijan, and elsewhere, suppressing resistance to collectivization required the intervention of the Red Army. Nevertheless, by 1932, almost two-thirds of peasant households had joined collectives, and by 1936, the figure was close to 90 percent. Collectivization ensured the regime control of the food supply. Forced to meet state procurement quotas even if they went hungry themselves, peasants received a pittance at most in return for their labor. In 1932–33, excessive state demand for grain led to man-made famines in Ukraine, the North Caucasus, the lower Volga, and Kazakhstan. Millions perished, the majority of them Ukrainians. This has led some to conclude that the Ukrainian famine was a deliberate act of genocide. For several years thereafter, rationing was instituted in cities and towns. Peasants never fully recovered from the trauma.

Although as wasteful of human and natural resources, and almost as reliant on coercion, the industrialization campaign was arguably more successful than collectivization. It also enjoyed more popular support.

State ownership and central planning of the entire economy replaced the uncertainties of the capitalist free market, enabling the regime to mobilize resources, human and material, as needed. The First Five Year plan, declared complete in 1932 after only four and a half years, placed greatest emphasis on heavy industry and energy production—coal, iron, steel, electricity—the bases for any modern industrial economy. The unreliability of Soviet statistics makes it virtually impossible to measure the extent of growth accurately. Nevertheless, and even if quantity often trumped quality, industrial growth was real: by the mid-1930s the Soviet Union had become an industrial power. Offering a marked contrast to a global economy still battered by depression, in which even capitalists harbored doubts about their system, Soviet-style state-sponsored economic development became a compelling alternative to capitalism. As developing nations freed themselves from capitalist imperialism, many would embrace the Soviet model.

Accomplished with considerable foreign expertise and equipment, but almost entirely without investment from abroad, Soviet economic modernization was built on the backs of workers and peasants. The unemployment that had dogged the lives of hundreds of thousands of workers since the early 1920s ended. Millions of peasants abandoned villages to take new jobs. Especially in hardship locations, labor was often compulsory, performed by convicts or "free" men and women ordered to the sites or forbidden to change jobs. Labor unions became powerless. Labor infractions such as lateness were harshly punished. Consumer goods were chronically in short supply; so was food. Nowhere was life easy. Migrants inundated cities; housing failed to keep pace. Anna Dubova, a skilled confectionary worker in Moscow with no place to live in the early 1930s, would spend the night with girlfriends. Marriage to a communist, who like other party members enjoyed privileged access to scarce goods, gained them a room of their own: "When I went to bed, I would think to myself, Dear Lord, I'm in my very own bed. I experienced such happiness; it was like being in seventh heaven, I was that happy."[7]

But economic change also vastly expanded opportunities for upward mobility, especially for people from a proper "proletarian" background. Popular education campaigns had already virtually eliminated illiteracy. Tens of thousands of workers and young communists (Komsomols) seized opportunities to pursue more advanced studies in night classes after a long day's work or, later in the 1930s, full-time with state support. Practical-minded men like Leonid Brezhnev, future head of the USSR, most often chose training in fields like engineering and technology that prepared them for administrative careers in the new economy.

Such opportunities were less accessible for women. While millions joined the wage labor force, most women worked a "double shift," doing housework at home after their day on the job. Day care expanded, but not nearly enough. Women, especially those with children, had little time to study. When the birthrate declined, instead of easing the pressures on women the regime tried to strengthen the family, in part by punishing sex outside of marriage. In 1934, homosexual acts between consenting males became a criminal offense. A new family law of 1936 made divorce more difficult and costly and outlawed abortion except when pregnancy threatened a woman's life or health. Financial incentives for having babies similar to those offered by Catholic countries and Nazi Germany were introduced. The law banning abortion was couched in the language of women's rights: "In no country in the world does woman enjoy such complete equality in all branches of political, social and family life as in the

The coalminer Aleksei Stakhanov, who earned acclaim in 1935 by greatly exceeding his daily work norm, explains his work methods to a co-worker. Workers who followed his example became known as Stakhanovites and were rewarded with higher wages and access to coveted scarce goods, evidence of the "good life" that was supposedly just over the horizon, under construction in the Soviet Union. Library of Congress, LC-USW33- 024256-C.

USSR," it proclaimed.[8] But the birthrate barely budged, largely due to illegal—and highly dangerous—abortions.

Now fully state controlled, modern mass communications—the press, radio, and cinema—trumpeted Soviet achievements across the country's vast expanses. Socialist realism, the ruling paradigm after 1934, governed the arts. Artists were required to depict reality not as it was, but as it would become in the radiant future. Borrowing techniques from Hollywood, Soviet musical comedies proved especially successful in combining the formula with popular appeal. Newspapers celebrated the cult of Stalin and the superiority of the Soviet system. The media highlighted the accomplishments of the industrialization drive: enormous building projects such as the Turkestan-Siberian Railroad; the construction of new industrial cities such as Magnitogorsk on the windswept steppe at the base of the Ural Mountains; the completion of Moscow's modern subway system; and the transformation of Moscow into a beacon for world socialism. Failures, when reported at all, were blamed on enemies: sabotage by "bourgeois" specialists or foreigners determined to destroy socialist achievements. News of the larger world was adapted to Soviet needs.

Fear of enemies and isolation from the outside world intensified in 1936, when the "terror" began. The most compelling interpretations of its causes note both real threats from abroad and imagined ones at home. In the West, Adolf Hitler spoke openly of his hatred for communism and his intent to expand eastward by force. In the Far East, a militarily aggressive Japan raised the specter of a war on two fronts. The threat prompted the morbidly suspicious Stalin, acting behind the scenes, to rid himself and Soviet society of anyone who might oppose him or aid the enemy in the event of war. The NKVD, successor to the Cheka, did the dirty work. Documents discovered in the archives after the collapse of the Soviet Union show that its work was guided by quotas for arrests and executions of "anti-Soviet elements," identified by type and region. The NKVD arrested suspects, and subjecting them to brutal tortures, extracted confessions of preposterous crimes. Party members became the first and best-known victims. In carefully staged show trials, men prominent in the party since Lenin's day confessed to outrageous acts—engaging in plots to murder Lenin and Stalin and overthrow the Soviet Union, becoming agents of enemy powers, and more.

As terror widened, people began to live in fear of midnight steps on the staircase. Some groups suffered more than others. After party members, most vulnerable were former "enemies," such as kulaks, nobles, and priests; people who thought for themselves like intellectuals and writers; members of "suspect" nationalities such as Germans, Poles, and Koreans; and anyone of foreign origin or with foreign ties, including political refugees escaping persecution in Germany, Italy, and Spain. The terror decimated the army high command. No one was safe except Stalin. Ordered to be "vigilant," to "unmask" hidden enemies, people learned to conceal their thoughts. Denunciations were encouraged and could be submitted anonymously. Some used the opportunity to settle old scores. Before it ground to a halt toward the end of 1938, the terror had swept up millions. Those not executed were sent to concentration camps (GULAGS—an acronym for *gosudarstvennye lageri*, or state camps), where they contributed significantly to the industrialization drive and might remain for decades. The chief beneficiary was Stalin, whose role few suspected. A younger generation, educated in Soviet schools and imbued with Stalinist values, also benefited. Replacing those who disappeared, they moved quickly into managerial and other responsible positions.

Despite the constant references to enemies, spies, and foreign threats in the media and at the workplace, when war arrived, it caught just about everyone by surprise. In August 1939, the Soviets had concluded a cynically titled "Non Aggression" pact with Nazi Germany. The aim: to enable the Soviet Union to stand aside while war between capitalist and fascist powers devastated both. Stalin took swift advantage of the pact's secret clauses, which permitted the Soviets to absorb parts of the tsarist empire lost after World War I: Estonia, Latvia, Lithuania, and Bessarabia plus the eastern portions of Poland, that is, the western portions of contemporary Ukraine and Belarus. These territories proved no obstacle, however, when Hitler's forces launched a surprise assault on the Soviet Union early on June 22, 1941.

Catching the leadership by surprise, the lightning attacks along three separate fronts proved stunningly effective, easily overrunning Soviet defenses and destroying much of the Soviet air force. The Germans quickly occupied much of the western borderlands, home to some 40 percent of Soviet industry, some 80 million citizens, and the majority of European Jews. By September 8, German forces had surrounded and placed under siege the city of Leningrad (formerly Petrograd, renamed for Lenin after his death). They got so close to Moscow in early October that, through their field glasses, German tank commanders could see the golden cupolas of the Kremlin glimmering in the sunlight. But the Germans failed to take Moscow—the first sign that the Soviet Union might withstand the onslaught.

Over the next three years, the Soviet Union absorbed virtually the entire brunt of the Nazi war machine's assault on the European front, with only the British still resisting there. Perhaps the fiercest of the many bloody battles occurred at Stalingrad, on the lower Volga. In late August 1942, carpet-bombing by German planes reduced the city to rubble and smoke and killed an estimated forty thousand civilians. Enduring unrelenting bombardment, Soviet defenders battled the invaders from block to block, ruin to ruin, on a front with no clear boundaries, and against what appeared to be overwhelming odds. They fought with extraordinary determination despite conditions that defied description. "What's around me is a very hell," a junior officer wrote to his wife, referring to the filth, the noise, the danger of falling shells.[9] Light wounds did not matter; virtually every Soviet soldier suffered them. The severely wounded often died where they lay. Only in November 1942, with the arrival of reinforcements, did the tide turn in favor of the Soviets. Even then, confronted with Hitler's refusal to allow surrender, the Germans fought on until February 2, 1943. The Soviet victory at Stalingrad, often viewed as the turning point of the war, cost an estimated half million Soviet lives. Soon after, Soviet forces began to take the offensive elsewhere, pushing the Germans westward, freeing the occupied territories of the Soviet Union and central-eastern Europe as they went. The conquest of Germany alone took another half million Soviet lives.

As it fought for its life, Stalin's regime exercised to the full its coercive powers. It punished as traitors, collectively, roughly two million non-Russian peoples, some of whose members collaborated with the enemy. First Germans, then Kalmyks and Crimean Tatars, and then Chechens, Ingush, and other Caucasian peoples were deported, in cattle trucks, to forced labor settlements in the east. Many died along the way. The regime threw soldiers into battle, careless of their lives. Soldiers who allowed themselves to be captured alive or retreated without permission of the high command were punished as traitors. Labor legislation became even more draconian. Civilians were ordered to work—at civil defense, digging anti-tank ditches, taking the place of those who left for war.

However, the war also highlighted the strengths of the Soviet system. The industrialization drive prepared the Soviets to wage war, successfully, against Europe's most advanced economy. Their centralized, top-down administration enabled them to maintain production despite German occupation of Soviet industrial centers. In the summer of 1941, the regime began the unprecedented feat of dis-assembling and transferring thousands of industrial enterprises and some 25 million workers and their families from west to east, beyond the Urals, safe from German forces, where they would make a key contribution to victory. By 1943, the Soviets were producing more tanks than their enemy. They also received tanks, fighter planes, and bombers from their temporary allies, the United States and Great Britain. The US Lend-Lease program went into high gear in 1943 and would contribute about $10 billion in equipment and supplies to the Soviet war effort. Lend-Lease Spam, a canned meat product from the United States that served as a significant source of war-time protein, was slyly known as "the Second Front," a comment on the Allies' failure to relieve German military pressure on the Soviet Union until late in the war.

Despite—perhaps even because of—its unspeakable horrors, the war also brought Soviet citizens a new sense of unity and purpose. The Germans waged a vicious war of extermination in the East. Aiming to destroy the USSR, wipe out communism, and turn Slavs into slaves, they treated the populations in conquered areas with stunning brutality. The regime responded by downplaying communist ideology and appealing to Russian nationalism. The Comintern was disbanded and in 1943, the Russian Orthodox Church officially rehabilitated. Repression tem-porarily eased, while scope for popular initiative increased. Millions volunteered for the military, women as well as men. By war's end, women constituted about 8 percent of the fighting forces as well as 56 percent of the labor force. Even the cult of Stalin came to serve a purpose: like Winston Churchill in England, Stalin inspired in his people the courage to resist.

Afterward, World War II—known in the Soviet Union as the "Great Patriotic War"—assumed a central place in the collective memory. Many of its survivors remembered it as the paramount experience of their lives. The war "restored the pride and dignity which the daily grind of a totalitarian, bureaucratic society had all but chipped away. The war made us a nation once again," remem-bered the nuclear physicist and future dissident Andrei Sakharov, merging the Soviet and national causes just as did wartime propa-ganda.[10] To the leadership, victory meant something else: the vindi-cation of their system.

CHAPTER 8

Cold War and the Collapse of Communism (1945 to the Present)

Victory over Germany transformed the Soviet Union into a superpower, one of only two in the postwar world. The Soviet Union's international status reached its zenith, and its territorial expanse became greater than ever. The USSR once again encompassed the Baltic Republics, Bessarabia, and the western portions of Ukraine and Belarus, territory gained through the Nazi-Soviet pact and now retained despite fierce local resistance, especially from Ukrainians. The expanded USSR covered about one-sixth of the globe. Its influence extended farther, over east-central Europe, which the Red Army liberated from German occupation.

The Soviet Union was, however, a superpower crippled by war. The price its people paid for victory remains virtually incalculable. So many lives were lost that Stalin, unwilling to reveal Soviet weakness, falsified the number of wartime casualties. Only forty years later did the public learn that 7 to 8 million soldiers and 19 million civilians died in the war. Estimates now run as high as 30 million deaths. Of these, some 2.2 million were Jews, roughly 40 percent of the Soviet Union's pre-war Jewish population, singled out for massacre by the Germans along with communists, homosexuals, the handicapped, and Gypsies. Millions more people returned from the battlefields maimed in mind or body, only to find devastation awaiting back home.

The fighting had destroyed one-third of the pre-war capital stock, including half of all railway lines. Hunger reigned in the innumerable devastated towns and villages through which war had passed "like a column of fire" in the words of the future dissident Lev Kopelev, once a true believer. "A piece of sugar was a thing of wonder, and the children, with their enormous eyes and their bluish-white faces, choked and chewed on some kind of mud-block, bitter bread made of the devil only knew what."[1] In 1946–47, famine raged.

The war had a completely different impact on the other super-power, the United States. During the war, the United States endured neither fighting nor bombing on its soil save for the Japanese attack on Pearl Harbor. World War II cost it fewer than half a million lives. At the end of the war, the US economy had become the strongest in the world. When, on August 6, 1945, US planes dropped an atomic bomb on Hiroshima and three days later, on Nagasaki, they upended the global balance of power and gained an immense advantage. It lasted until 1949, when the Soviets tested their own atomic bomb, initiating an arms race that devoured enormous resources on both sides and, at its height, seemed to threaten all humanity with annihilation.

Whether the "Cold War" that erupted between the two powers was inevitable and which side was mainly to blame for it are questions that remain unresolved. What is clear is that profound ideological differences and mutual suspicions led each to interpret the others' actions in the worst possible light and react accordingly. The fate of east-central Europe became the primary bone of contention in the immediate post-war years. Regarding Soviet security against a possible German threat as paramount, Stalin insisted on "friendly" governments in the region the Soviets controlled. He then partially reconstructed their systems along Soviet lines. To Stalin's former allies, these developments confirmed fears of an expansionist "communist menace" that had to be stopped. Warned Britain's wartime leader, Winston Churchill, in 1946, "From Stettin in the Baltic to Trieste in the Adriatic an iron curtain has descended across the Continent."[2]

A year later, President Harry Truman committed the United States to support opponents of communism anywhere in the world, instituted a loyalty test for government workers to ferret out communists, and offered Europeans massive US aid, in the form of the Marshall Plan. The Marshall Plan's goal: to restore devastated European economies, encourage US-style consumer-capitalism, and eliminate the lure of communism, with its promises of equality and social justice. Moscow responded by ousting the remaining moderates from east-central European governments, consolidating Communist Party rule, repressing real and imagined opposition, and fully imposing Soviet style systems. After 1947, the momentum of the Cold War seemed irreversible.

As nations in Africa, Asia, and the Caribbean freed themselves from European colonial domination, the Cold War became a global struggle. Both the United States and USSR sought to draw newly independent states into its orbit. Stalin proceeded cautiously. In China, the triumph of communists led by Mao Zedong was an outcome that the United States worked hard to prevent and the Soviet Union did little to encourage. Moscow nevertheless welcomed Mao's victory as a foretaste of the future for the colonized peoples of Asia. The Korean War heightened Cold War tensions. In 1950, Kim Il Sung, the North Korean communist leader, initiated the invasion of US-backed South Korea with Stalin's reluctant consent, but with only Chinese military support. Fought against the United Nations' troops on the ground, the Korean War was the first of many in which client states, on their own initiative, drew the superpowers that backed them into conflicts, sometimes threatening a broader, nuclear confrontation.

The Cold War shaped domestic as well as foreign policies. It absorbed Soviet resources and forced the leadership to choose between guns and butter. To ensure peace, the Soviet people were told, they must be prepared for war. Faced with reconstructing the devastated economy, Soviet planners embraced the usual priorities: heavy industry and defense, which absorbed roughly a quarter of the postwar budget. By 1950, heavy industry had not only recovered but even surpassed pre-war levels. Everyday life had also begun to improve, if unevenly. *New York Times* reporter Harrison Salisbury, returning to Moscow in 1949 after a five-year absence, was impressed by the changes he saw: the people looked healthier, construction crews labored everywhere, food was ample, and some consumer goods, such as aluminum pots and pans, were not only available but of better quality than before. Scarcities continued to burden the population, however: Salisbury once witnessed women rioting outside a store selling hard-to-get carpet material. And the regime neglected key priorities. To replace wartime losses, it desperately wanted women, even unmarried women, to bear as many children as possible and changed the laws to encourage reproduction; however, it failed to provide decent health care. Shortages of medical personnel and such basic supplies as gloves and soap plagued maternity clinics and hospitals. Childcare became less available in the postwar years than during the final years of war.

Cold War tensions also exacerbated the xenophobia that had shaped politics even before the war. Soviet society was almost entirely shut off from the larger world. Foreign news, foreign products, foreign people all became subject to the most stringent controls. Only the most sympathetic foreigners gained permission to visit, and a 1947 law forbade them to marry Soviet citizens. Soviet soldiers who had fought in eastern Europe and been amazed to find superior standards of living even in war-ravaged societies, were, on their return strictly prohibited from discussing what they had seen. Everything associated with the West received negative treatment. Mary Leder, a resident of Moscow at the time, remembered, "Each day brought fresh newspaper reports of American 'crimes.' The Western powers were accused of locking up and preventing Soviet citizens in displaced persons camps from returning home. A publishing house in Moscow was chastised for publishing a translation of an American book on U. S. political parties and was accused of manufacturing propaganda for enemy ideology."[3] Ideological guidelines tightened; writers and artists fell into line or fell silent.

The Russian nation was celebrated as never before. Propaganda praised everything Russian and gave Russians credit for inventing all manner of technological innovations—the electric lamp, the telephone, the airplane, and more. "Cosmopolitanism" became a dirty word. It reflected the growing association of "enemies" with ethnic rather than class criteria and the crackdown on all nationalist sentiment except Russian. In the spring and summer of 1949, nearly 100,000 alleged "counterrevolutionaries" and their families were deported from the newly annexed Baltic Republics, so as to crush resistance to Sovietization. But campaigns against cosmopolitanism focused mainly on Jews. In 1948, when the Jewish community joyfully welcomed the Russian-born Golda Meir, Israel's new ambassador to Moscow, the simmering anti-Semitism of the postwar period became overt. The authorities publicly attacked prominent Jews. Many lost their jobs; dozens were imprisoned. The great actor Solomon Mikhoels, who as a member of the Jewish Anti-Fascist Committee had raised funds in the United States for the Soviet war effort, was murdered on Stalin's orders.

Official anti-Semitism represented a dramatic reversal for a state that, in contrast to the imperial regime, had formerly encouraged Jewish culture and provided individuals of Jewish background with unprecedented opportunities for upward mobility. Early in 1953, newspapers proclaimed the uncovering of a "Doctors' Plot," according to which prominent physicians, the majority Jewish, planned to poison Stalin. People feared the news heralded another round of terror. If so, Stalin's death on March 5, 1953, prevented it. Despite the horrors his rule had visited on so many, millions of people wept in grief over his death, concentration camp prisoners among them.

The system did not survive the man, or at least, not completely. Even before a new leader had emerged from among them, the men in Stalin's circle sought to limit his excesses—the extensive use of coercion and terror that threatened even those at the top, including themselves;

ПОД ВОДИТЕЛЬСТВОМ ВЕЛИКОГО СТАЛИНА—ВПЕРЕД К КОММУНИЗМУ!

"Under the Leadership of the Great Stalin—Forward to Communism" reads the caption beneath this propaganda poster of 1951. With a map of the Soviet Union in the background, and the smiling peoples of its various nationalities gazing in adoration at Stalin, the poster demonstrates visually the hierarchical character of Soviet nationality policy. Courtesy of the Russian and Soviet Poster Collection, Hoover Institution Archives, Stanford, California.

extravagant and wasteful projects; concentration on military production; and neglect of consumer goods and human needs. Cultural controls eased. In 1954, Ilya Ehrenburg's novel *The Thaw* gave its name to the era. It featured harsh criticism of the ruling elite, depicted as personifying the Soviet system. Tens of thousands of prisoners were released from the camps, as were the accused in the "Doctors' Plot." Some ethnic groups deported before and during the war, such as the Chechen, Ingush, and Kalmyk peoples, regained their legal rights and subsequently were permitted to return to their territory. Deportees from the western portions of the USSR received amnesties, too, although some had engaged in armed resistance to Soviet power. Within three years of Stalin's death, perhaps a million prisoners had returned from the camps. The press made no mention of it.

Change accelerated in 1956. By then, the earthy and loquacious Nikita Khrushchev had triumphed in the power struggle that followed Stalin's death. Born in 1894 to an impoverished peasant family and barely educated, Khrushchev, who had begun to work at the age of fourteen, was a beneficiary of the party's policy of recruiting and promoting workers such as he. Proud of the revolution's accomplishments, Khrushchev sought to reignite its enthusiasms and end Stalinera violence. His moment came at the end of the Twentieth Congress of the Communist Party in February 1956. Speaking before a stunned audience in a closed session, Khrushchev openly criticized aspects of Stalin's rule for the first time. Deploring the terror of the late 1930s, Khrushchev detailed the arrest, torture, and forced confession of loyal party members. Stalin, he declared, facilitated the use "of the cruelest repression, violating all norms of revolutionary legality, against anyone who in any way disagreed with Stalin, against those who were only suspected of hostile intent, against those who had bad reputations." Khrushchev challenged the idea that genuine "enemies" had threatened the system. "Many entirely innocent individuals—who in the past had defended the party line—became victims."[4]

At the same time, Khrushchev's speech affirmed the correctness of other Stalinist policies, including industrialization and collectivization. It also referred only to the sufferings of party members, blamed everything on Stalin, and left much unsaid, including the horrific human costs of collectivization and liquidation of kulaks. It was nevertheless a bombshell. Despite efforts to preserve its secrecy (it remained unpublished in the Soviet Union until 1989), it soon became known abroad. It led to unrest in Poland and an attempted revolution in Hungary. The Hungarians proclaimed neutrality and withdrew from the Warsaw Pact, which was the Soviets' response to the North Atlantic Treaty Organization (NATO). Blaming the Hungarian uprising on the West, Soviet tanks rolled in and crushed it. Yet politics had really changed. When Hungarian unrest spilled over into the Baltic republics, student leaders were neither deported nor killed but expelled from school or given warnings. Violence ceased to be the cornerstone of Soviet rule.

A newly confident Soviet Union became more open to the outside world. In 1957, Moscow hosted the World Youth Festival, bringing to the city tens of thousands of young people from all over the globe. Soviet youth savored their first contact with foreigners. "Day and night people thronged the boulevards in national costumes, with instruments, with flowers, with arms full of gifts. The Russians threw themselves into this festival as if every stranger were a kinsman, returning home," remembered Kim Chernin, who traveled from the United States to attend.[5] Together with foreign guests, Soviet youth danced all night to the sounds of jazz and African drums, and listened to open-air poetry readings.

The American National Exhibition staged in Moscow's Sokolniki Park in 1959 offered Soviets a glimpse of American life. Designed to tempt Soviet citizens with the consumer delights of capitalism, the exhibition—a "soft" front in the Cold War—included a "typical" American home, complete with a full-sized modern kitchen, stocked with gleaming pots and pans and modern appliances. Over its six-week run, some 2.7 million Soviet citizens visited the exhibition. Although some visitors came away impressed, others expressed confidence in their own system. Their comments echoed Khrushchev's pledge that in the near future, the Soviet Union would catch up with and overtake the West and attain a communist state of plenty. "You have achieved this in 150 years. We shall achieve it without fail in 50, this means our *Soviet* way of life is better," wrote a visitor in the exhibition's guestbook.[6]

Indeed, in key spheres of Cold War competition, the Soviet Union appeared to surge ahead. In 1957, the launching of Sputnik, the first artificial earth satellite, became a source of anxiety to the US government and pride to Soviet citizens. In 1961, the Soviet Union sent the first manned craft into outer space. The "Columbus of Space," Yurii Gagarin, was a model Soviet citizen. He grew up on a collective farm and worked in a factory, learning to fly on weekends before being drafted into the military. Handsome, fiercely patriotic, perpetually smiling, he became the most famous figure in Soviet public life. Valentina Tereshkova followed him into space two years later. Daughter of a tractor driver, herself a textile worker and party activist, Tereshkova likewise symbolized Soviet success, especially in the advancement of women as well as workers.

Even the provision of consumer goods improved, although the Soviet Union still lagged behind the United States in this sphere of competition. The rate of housing construction nearly doubled in Khrushchev's time. New high-rise apartment buildings sprang up on the outskirts of cities, displacing villages and farms. Equipped with kitchen, bath, and one or two rooms, the apartments represented a vast improvement over the communal quarters where most urban people lived, even if the buildings were so hastily and shoddily built that they quickly acquired the nickname "khrushchoby," or Khrushchev's slums. Shoes, clothing, domestic appliances, and furniture became more readily available. So did places in day care, although never enough to meet the demand.

The regime proved less successful in its efforts to address chronic problems in agriculture, the stepchild of planners since collectivization. Khrushchev launched the Virgin Lands campaign, an attempt to put under cultivation vast stretches of the Kazakh steppe and

During a 1959 tour, the first visit to the United States by a Soviet leader, Nikita Khrushchev was impressed by the barnyard and burgeoning cornfields of Iowa farmer Raymond Garst. When he returned to Moscow, Khrushchev pressed for the extensive planting of corn in Russia's unsuitable conditions. The corn campaign proved a disaster, another of the "hare-brained schemes" that would eventually cost Khrushchev his leadership. Wisconsin Historical Society, Image ID 11243.

western Siberia, but also to reanimate revolutionary enthusiasm by relying on young volunteers. After impressive initial results, however, the land became exhausted, with millions of tons of topsoil lost to erosion. An initiative to compensate collective farmers for the actual cost of their products led, in 1962, to a rise in meat and dairy prices. Accustomed to food prices kept artificially low by government subsidies, the public reacted with outrage, and riots broke out. The worst occurred in Novocherkassk in the north Caucasus, where factory pay had just fallen by about 30 percent. Several thousand workers and their supporters marched peacefully in protest, only to be fired on by government troops when they refused to disperse. Dozens were wounded and more than twenty people killed. Not a word appeared in the press. Thereafter, the price of bread and other products remained unchanged for decades, even though agricultural productivity remained low, so low that in 1963, the authorities imported grain from abroad.

Cultural policy presented another dilemma for Khrushchev's regime. Stalinist-style rigidity clearly had to go, but what would replace it? Eager for greater openness and honesty in the arts and more attention to the individual, artists and intellectuals tested the limits of the possible. When Boris Pasternak's novel *Doctor Zhivago*, having been rejected by Soviet publications, was published abroad and won the Nobel Prize for literature in 1958, Khrushchev launched a bitter campaign against the writer. Pasternak, however, avoided punishment, an unimaginable outcome in Stalin's time. Then in 1962, Khrushchev oversaw a second "thaw." Stalin's corpse was removed from its place of honor in the Lenin mausoleum. A special commission prepared three volumes treating Stalin's crimes. "We must tell the truth about that period," declared Khrushchev. "Future generations will judge us, so let them know what conditions we had to work under, what sort of legacy we inherited."[7] Khrushchev personally approved the publication of Alexander Solzhenitsyn's short novel *One Day in the Life of Ivan Denisovitch*. Depicting the horrors of concentration camp life as experienced by a simple peasant, Solzhenitsyn's work became a popular sensation.

Khrushchev's associates did not all support his comparatively liberal policy. They also condemned some of his other initiatives, among them the Virgin Lands campaign, as "hare-brained." Yet it was Khrushchev's missteps in international affairs that brought his leading role to an end. Committed to a policy of "peaceful coexistence" with the United States and to the easing of Cold War tensions, Khrushchev hoped to redirect resources from the military to human needs. His actions, however, too often belied his words. He proved more prone to take risks than Stalin, and also faced competition from communist China, by the late 1950s no longer an ally but a rival for the loyalties of post-colonial states. Moscow secretly sent to its ally, newly communist Cuba, nuclear missiles capable of reaching the United States. US aerial reconnaissance soon detected them. On October 22, 1962, President John F. Kennedy responded with an ultimatum: either the Soviets could withdraw their missiles or they would face nuclear war. Confronted with the unthinkable, Khrushchev withdrew the missiles, in a humiliating and highly public defeat. Two years later, his rivals in the leadership ousted him, but they did so peacefully, evidence of the changes Khrushchev himself had overseen. He was neither shot nor imprisoned, but instead forced into "retirement"—at his own request, or so the public was told. Few mourned his fall.

Thereafter, efforts to revive revolutionary fervor and achieve communism ceased. The men who replaced Khrushchev sought stability, not change. Leonid Brezhnev, the leading figure by the end of the 1960s, was typical. Born in 1906 to a working-class family, a party member from 1929, he belonged to the first generation to have lived their entire adult lives in the Soviet Union. Technological training prepared such men for managerial careers and rapid advancement in the 1930s, filling posts emptied by the terror. Conservative in orientation—an odd term to use for leaders of a regime originating in revolution—they were not about to shake up the system. Criticism of Stalin ended, as did efforts at reform. Cultural controls tightened, freezing the "thaw" in literary expression.

Yet Soviet interaction with the West increased, motivated in part by the Soviets' need to remain abreast of scientific and technological advances. Foreign exchange students and scholars, foreign tourists, foreign goods, and selected foreign films grew more commonplace, especially in Moscow and Leningrad. They offered temptations to young people, less likely to share their parents' pride in Soviet accomplishments. Young people's desire for consumer goods (jeans, especially), rock music, and other products of the capitalist world troubled the regime and created a generation gap similar to that in Europe and the United States.

While terror did not return, fear did. Soviet citizens had to be careful what they wrote or said in public, especially after 1966 when disseminating "anti-Soviet slander" became a crime. Around the kitchen table and among trusted friends and relatives one could speak one's mind—but only after removing the telephone, which just might be bugged. Events abroad reinforced political orthodoxy at home. In 1968, reformers in communist Czechoslovakia attempted to institute "socialism with a human face," abolishing censorship and moving toward a multiparty system. Fearful that these ideas might prove contagious, the Soviets and their East European allies intervened, crushing the "Prague Spring." The invasion horrified Soviet intellectuals who nurtured hopes for further reform at home, and a handful of them dared to protest by demonstrating in Red Square. The authorities arrested them immediately. The protestors were part of a small but persistent dissident movement. Advocating reform of the system and protection of human rights, a thorn in the side of the authorities, they acted as the conscience of their society. Andrei Sakharov became one of the most visible campaigners. A member of the prestigious Academy of Sciences, a father of the Soviet atomic bomb, Sakharov proved an influential opponent of nuclear proliferation. In recognition of his efforts, in 1975 Sakharov won the Nobel Peace prize. Five years later he endured exile to the city of Gorky, punishment for his protest against the Soviet invasion of Afghanistan.

Yet many Soviet people welcomed the stability of what the regime now called "developed socialism." Among the benefits were full employment and security in one's job, even if that job was sometimes boring and poorly paid. Subsidized by the state, the cost of housing, food, and other goods remained low, as did the price of public transport, health care, education, and a range of recreation and vacation facilities. If cheap consumer goods and welfare also meant persistent shortages and long lines for a wide range of products, including everyday items like toilet paper, they nevertheless seemed a genuine achievement for people whose forebears were impoverished peasants. A thriving black market somewhat eased the shortages for those who had money or the requisite personal contacts. Highly placed party members, outstanding artists, writers, and others of noteworthy achievement enjoyed privileged access to scarce goods. Access also depended on where you lived—Moscow, the showcase city, was the best supplied. Collective farmers in distant villages, who might even lack electricity, were at a severe disadvantage. On weekends, out-of-town shoppers crowded trains to and from Moscow.

The shortages were particularly hard on women, who, if married, juggled full-time employment and housework with little support from their husbands. The persistent dilemma of the "double burden" became public in 1969, when Natalia Baranskaya published a story, "A Week like Any Other," in the liberal journal *New World*. Featuring a harried wife and mother of two children with a demanding job, Baranskaya offered a vivid portrait of the everyday challenges faced by urban women—long lines, inadequate day care, husbands reluctant to share domestic duties, always having to rush, never having enough time, plus an impatient employer tired of hearing excuses. The heroine returns from work, carrying food bought on her lunch hour:

> At last my stop, Sokol. People jump up and rush up the narrow stairs. But I can't, I have milk and eggs in my bags. I flounder at the back of the queue. When I get to the bus stop there's a queue big enough to fill six buses. Should I try to get on to a full one? What about my bags? I try to squeeze on to the third. Because of bags in both my hands I can't hold on, one leg falls down from the high step, my knee gets knocked and hurt. At this moment the bus starts to move. Everyone cries out. I shriek, and some old man, standing by the door, grabs me and drags me in. I collapse on top of my bags.[8]

If revolutionary élan was evident anywhere in the 1970s, it was in the decolonizing world. This became the primary sphere of competition between the United States and the USSR. Leftward leaning leaders of emerging nations sought and obtained support from Moscow. To Western eyes, communism seemed on the march. In Vietnam, the communist-led north triumphed over the US-backed south, with Soviet assistance. The Soviets also supported communist regimes in Ethiopia and Nicaragua. But leftist leaders usually preferred to set their own course and in any case, communist states had long ceased to be unified. In 1969, Soviet relations with China deteriorated to the point of armed conflict along the Xinjiang-Kirghiz border. Then, in 1979, the Soviets severely damaged their own credibility as a supporter of national liberation. Intervening on behalf of communist revolutionaries in Afghanistan, Soviet forces became mired in a costly and protracted civil war. With the United States underwriting Muslim resistance, the war in Afghanistan appeared to destroy all hope for détente.

The Soviet Union collapsed little more than a decade later, surprising virtually everyone. Taking power in 1985, Mikhail Gorbachev tried mightily to reform and revitalize the Soviet system, as well as to end the Cold War. At fifty-four, he was the youngest Soviet leader in decades and unlike the ineffective and aging technocrats who preceded him, Gorbachev had trained in the law. A believer in the socialist system, his policies of *perestroika* (restructuring the almost stagnant economy), and *glasnost'* (openness) eventually created as many problems as they solved. *Glasnost'* aimed to create the openness needed to discuss and resolve pressing social and economic problems. Instead, it helped to undermine faith in the socialist system. Disillusionment accelerated after 1986, when a devastating nuclear accident occurred at the Chernobyl power station in Ukraine. As radioactive dust spewed into the atmosphere, Soviet citizens initially learned of the disaster from Western sources, not their own government.

After Chernobyl, state control of information greatly eased, while journalists and writers pressed the boundaries of the permissible to the limit and beyond. Television, journals, and newspapers informed a horrified and fascinated public about virtually every negative aspect of the Soviet past and present—the human cost of collectivization, the abuses of Stalinism, even the shortcomings of the hitherto sacred Lenin. At the same time, *perestroika* foundered. Aiming to create a more efficient economy that met consumer needs without abandoning key elements of the socialist system, the policy sought but failed to find a middle road between centralized planning and the capitalist free market. By early

1991, shortages had grown so severe that rationing was introduced for essential products such as sugar.

In the political realm, too, Gorbachev unleashed forces that he proved unable and eventually, unwilling, to control. By contrast with his predecessors, Gorbachev was hesitant to use force to maintain control of the east-central European satellite states or to back their unpopular rulers. Freed from the heavy hand of Moscow, their peoples chose their own path. In 1989, Germans destroyed the Berlin wall, constructed in 1961 to prevent East Germans from fleeing westward. Thereafter, one after another communist government succumbed to popular, "velvet" revolutions, most of them non-violent. The Soviets did not intervene.

At home, Gorbachev was equally hesitant to employ repression. Instead, he tried to introduce greater democracy into the Soviet system, in which he continued to believe. At the Nineteenth Party Conference in June 1988—the first such Conference to be televised—he called for popular elections for a new institution, the Congress of People's Deputies, which would govern alongside the Communist Party. Although the party retained the right to choose a third of the deputies, the remainder were to be elected by secret ballot. Organizations other than the party chose the candidates and some, including Andrei Sakharov, were not party members. The elections, which ended the Communist Party's monopoly on political power, galvanized the public, which for the first time since 1917 gained a genuine say in the selection of their representatives.

These political reforms, however, weakened the ties that bound together the republics of the Soviet Union. Communist Party members, with vested interest in maintaining their power, ruled them all. After Stalin's death, the republics enjoyed a kind of federalism that allowed them to express their national character in limited ways, such as folk music, art and ethnography, and education in the titular language. The renewal of Soviet-style affirmative action also opened opportunities for members of the designated nationality to advance within their republic's communist party (only the Russian republic lacked one) and state bureaucracy. Inadvertently, these policies encouraged a kind of national identity and fostered self-interest among some of the republics' leadership. In the non-Russian republics, the policy of *glasnost'* allowed long-simmering popular dissatisfaction with Soviet rule to burst into the open. As Moscow's control weakened, movements for national self-determination grew increasingly assertive. The first to break away were the Baltic republics, which had been forcibly incorporated into the Soviet Union following World War II after several decades of independence. By 1990, Estonia, Latvia, and Lithuania had effectively become separate nation-states.

Other republics began moving in the same direction. Among them were the republics of the South Caucasus—Armenia, Azerbaijan, and Georgia. In these as in others, however, movements for national

"No to Atomic Warfare," reads the sign carried by the Kazakh woman in the foreground, at the demonstration staged by the Nevada-Semipalatinsk Anti-Nuclear movement at the Soviet Union's nuclear test site in Kazakhstan, held on August 6, 1989, the forty-fourth anniversary of the bombing of Hiroshima. Named to show solidarity with similar anti-nuclear movements in the United States, in 1991 the movement succeeded in closing the Semipalatinsk testing site. Courtesy of Dmitrii Kalmykov and the EcoMuseum of Kazakhstan, and of Magdalena Stawkowski.

autonomy were complicated by the presence of other national minorities in the same republic, who often also pressed for greater rights. Perhaps the most dramatic conflict between nationalities occurred early in 1988, in the South Caucasus, where Armenians in the mountainous Karabakh region, part of Azerbaijan, took to the streets to agitate for a merger with Armenia. The Azerbaijanis responded with demonstrations in defense of their territorial integrity. Tensions escalated; violence broke out, with Azerbaijanis massacring Armenians in the towns of Sumgait and Baku.

Yielding to the demands for greater autonomy by the various republic leaders, Gorbachev, elected president of the Soviet Union by the Congress of People's Deputies, agreed to a new union treaty. However, before it could be signed in August 1991, party conservatives attempted to seize power. Aiming to preserve the old order, the conservatives instead contributed to its end. Boris Yeltsin, newly elected president of the Russian Federation, played a prominent role in the successful resistance, standing on a tank to rally support. He became a popular hero, far more popular than Gorbachev, who was on vacation in the Crimea at the time of the attempted coup. Accusing the Communist Party of collaborating with the conservatives, Yeltsin dissolved it. Then in December, after months of fruitless efforts to agree on a successor organization to the Soviet Union, Yeltsin met with the leaders of Ukraine and Belarus, who agreed to form the Commonwealth of Independent States. Abolishing the Soviet Union, the agreement transformed its constituent republics into separate states. Russia was left roughly the same size as in the late seventeenth century.

The change, however, made many unhappy and left fundamental issues unresolved. Among them were the rights of ethnic minorities within the newly independent states, and the fate of Russians residing there who, virtually overnight, found themselves living abroad. Although the breakup of the Soviet Union occurred relatively peacefully, competition over the rights of ethnic minorities eventually led to conflicts. Chechnya's demands for greater local autonomy prompted invasions by Russia in 1994 and 1999. Disputes over territorial and other issues have led to friction between Russia and former members of the USSR, including Georgia and Ukraine.

The collapse of the Soviet Union had global ramifications. The Cold War over, the United States became the sole superpower. Former client states, like Cuba, had to find other patrons or adjust to the new circumstances. The east-central European states that had been in the

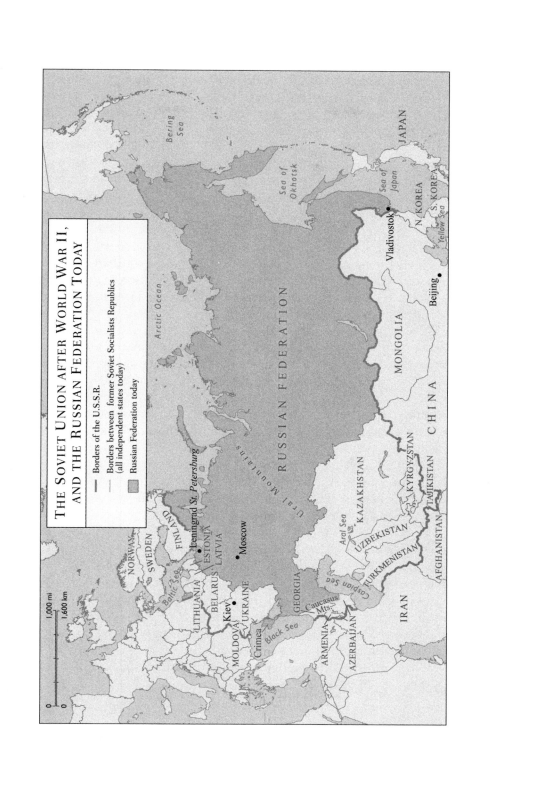

The Soviet Union after World War II, and the Russian Federation Today

— Borders of the U.S.S.R.

— Borders between former Soviet Socialists Republics
  (all independent states today)

☐ Russian Federation today

1,000 mi

1,600 km

NORWAY

SWEDEN

FINLAND

Baltic Sea

Leningrad St. Petersburg

ESTONIA

LATVIA

LITHUANIA

BELARUS

Kiev

UKRAINE

MOLDOVA

Crimea

Black Sea

Moscow

Ural Mountains

RUSSIAN FEDERATION

GEORGIA

Caucasus Mts.

ARMENIA

AZERBAIJAN

Caspian Sea

Aral Sea

KAZAKHSTAN

UZBEKISTAN

TURKMENISTAN

KYRGYZSTAN

TAJIKISTAN

AFGHANISTAN

IRAN

Arctic Ocean

Bering Sea

Sea of Okhotsk

Sea of Japan

JAPAN

N. KOREA

S. KOREA

Yellow Sea

Vladivostok

Beijing

MONGOLIA

CHINA

Soviet orbit joined NATO, an organization originally formed to block Soviet expansion; the new Baltic nations joined also.

Within Russia, too, dramatic changes occurred as the economy underwent major restructuring. Guided by foreign advisors, the new regime used "shock therapy" to convert the centrally owned and managed socialist economy into a free market system. In the process, state assets were sold to well-connected "businessmen" at bargain basement prices in one of the biggest giveaways in human history. Insiders gained a fortune; just about everyone else experienced a dramatic decline in living standards that lasted for years. However, recently, thanks in part to the revenue from oil exports, a new urban middle class has begun to emerge, even as dreadful poverty persists, especially among the elderly and in rural areas. A younger generation—urban, well educated, often well traveled, and able to access information easily through the Internet—nurtures expectations for an enhanced role in public life and respect for legal rights.

Whether the KGB-trained Vladimir Putin, who came to power in 1999, or those who succeed him, will manage to fend off such aspirations remains a question. They will confront many of the same challenges that their predecessors faced: how to govern a highly diverse population dwelling in a huge geographic area; how to reestablish and maintain a leading role in international affairs; and how to exploit both for export and internal use Russia's natural resources, including newly accessible resources in the Arctic and Siberia.

Putin has addressed them by adopting many of the methods used by his late tsarist and Soviet predecessors. Rejecting the West as a model for Russian politics, he has emphasized Russian nationalism despite Russia's multiethnic populace. To generate support for himself and his policies, Putin, having jettisoned communist ideology, has promoted the Russian Orthodox Church and Russia's unique path. He has strengthened the state and reduced the scope of civil society, dashing hopes for genuine democracy at least in the near future. Newly assertive in international politics, Russia has even turned to its former enemy China to counteract US power, in an echo of Cold War rivalries without the nuclear saber rattling. The challenges notwithstanding, Russia, bestriding the Eurasian subcontinent, is likely to remain a formidable power regardless of whether Putin's system survives the man.

Chronology

8TH CENTURY BCE–9TH CENTURY CE
Successive Iranian- and Turkic-speaking
peoples occupy the Black Sea steppe

6TH–8TH CENTURIES
Migrations of East Slavs from
Central Europe into regions of
modern Ukraine, Belarus, and
northwestern Russia

9TH CENTURY
Pechenegs occupy the Black Sea steppe

862
Legendary invitation to Ryurik to
rule Rus

980–1598
Exclusive Ryurikid dynasty rule over
Kievan Rus, Muscovy

988
Conversion of lands of Rus to
Christianity by Prince Vladimir

1054
Testament issued by Yaroslav the Wise
(approximate); church schism dividing
the eastern (Orthodox) and western
(Roman) branches of Christianity

1061
Qïpchaqs, having moved into the Black
Sea steppe, conduct their first attack on
Kievan Rus

1237–40
Mongol invasion and conquest of the
lands of Kievan Rus

1317
Mongol confirmation of the first prince
from Moscow, Yurii Danilovich, as
grand prince of Vladimir

1352
Black Death reaches northern Rus lands

1380
Battle of Kulikovo

1478
Muscovy annexes Novgorod

1497
Sudebnik (law code), including the
first universal restrictions on peasant
mobility, issued by Grand Prince Ivan III

1547
Ivan IV crowned Tsar and Grand Prince
of Muscovy

1552
Muscovy annexes Khanate of Kazan

1553
English discover White Sea route to
Muscovy

1558–83
Livonian War

1581–84
Yermak conquers Sibir for Muscovy

1598–1613
Time of Troubles

JULY 21, 1613
Michael Romanov crowned tsar

1613–1917
Romanov dynasty rules Muscovy,
Russian Empire

1649
Adoption of law code (*ulozhenie*), final
stage of enserfment of peasantry

1654–67
Thirteen Years' War between Muscovy
and Poland-Lithuania resulting in
annexation of eastern Ukraine and Kiev
by Muscovy

1666–67
Church council condemns Old Believers, deposes Patriarch Nikon

1669–71
Stenka Razin rebellion

1721
Treaty of Nystadt secures Russian access to Baltic Sea; Tsar Peter (the Great) is declared emperor

1725–62
Palace Guards exercise sway over a series of weak rulers; noble privileges increase; rights of peasant serfs diminish

1768–74
Russo-Turkish War; Russia incorporates territory North of Black Sea

1773–75
Pugachev uprising

1772–95
Russia takes over Crimean Khanate; Poland partitioned between Russia, Prussia, and Austria; Russia annexes eastern sectors of Poland, including portions of Ukraine and Belarus

1812–14
Russia triumphs in war against Napoleon and participates decisively at Congress of Vienna (1814–15)

DECEMBER 1825
Decembrist revolt against autocracy

1853–56
Crimean War

1859–64
Resistance led by Imam Shamil in North Caucasus defeated (1859); conquest of West Caucasus

1861–74
Era of Great Reforms, including abolition of serfdom, creation of *zemstvo* and new judicial system, and democratization of military conscription

1865–81
Conquest of Central Asia

MARCH 1, 1881
Revolutionary terrorists assassinate Tsar Alexander II

1891–1903
Construction of Trans-Siberian railway

1904–05
Russo-Japanese War

1905
Popular revolution wins expanded civil liberties and a limited representative body, the Duma

1914–18
World War I

FEBRUARY 23–MARCH 2, 1917
Popular unrest forces abdication of Tsar Nicholas II

OCTOBER 24–26, 1917
October Revolution; the Bolsheviks seize power

1918–21
Civil war with Whites, and intervention by foreign powers; the Bolsheviks, now called communists, emerge triumphant and retain control over most of pre-war Russian empire

1922
Union of Soviet Socialist Republics is founded

JANUARY 24, 1924
Communist leader Vladimir Il'ich Lenin dies

1929–33
First Five Year Plan initiates rapid industrialization and forcible collectivization

1936–38
Terror affects countless individuals, and decimates the ranks of the Communist Party, as well as intellectual, military, professional, and ethnic elites

AUGUST 1939
The Nazi-Soviet "Non-Aggression" Pact

1941–45
"Great Patriotic War" devastates Soviet cities and villages, and takes the lives of at least 27 million people

MARCH 5, 1946
Winston Churchill's "Iron Curtain" speech

MARCH 5, 1953
Death of Stalin

1956
Nikita Khrushchev attacks Stalin in "Secret Speech"; popular uprisings break out in Poland and Hungary

APRIL 12, 1961
Yurii Gagarin becomes first man in space

OCTOBER 22–28, 1962
Cuban Missile Crisis brings world to brink of nuclear war

1968
Communist bloc troops enter Czechoslovakia, crushing of "Prague Spring"

1985
Mikhail Gorbachev introduces *glasnost'* and *perestroika*

1986
Chernobyl nuclear accident

1991
The Soviet Union ceases to exist

2000, 2004, 2012
Vladimir Putin elected president of Russia

Notes

PREFACE

1. http://soviethistory.macalester.edu/index.php?page=article&ArticleID=1991resign1&SubjectID=1991end&Year=1991

CHAPTER 1

1. *Polnoe Sobranie Russkikh Letopisei*, vol. 1, *Lavrent'evskaia letopis'* (Moscow: Iazyki Russkoi Kul'tury, 1997), 19–20, trans. based on *The Russian Primary Chronicle. Laurentian Text*, trans. and ed. Samuel Hazzard Cross and Olgerd P. Sherbowitz-Wetzor. Mediaeval Academy of America Publication, no. 60 (Cambridge, MA: Mediaeval Academy of America, 1953), 59–60.

2. Aḥmad Ibn Faḍlān, *Ibn Fadlan's Journey to Russia: A Tenth-Century Traveler from Baghad to the Volga River,* trans. Richard Nelson Frye (Princeton, NJ: Markus Wiener, 2005), 63.

3. Constantine Porphyrogenitus, *De Administrando Imperio*, Greek text ed. Gy. Moravcsik, English trans. R. J. H. Jenkins (Washington, DC: Dumbarton Oaks, Center for Byzantine Studies, 1967), 59, 63.

4. *Russian Primary Chronicle*, 183.

5. *De Administrando Imperio*, 51.

6. *Russian Primary Chronicle*, 116–117.

7. *Russian Primary Chronicle*, 56.

8. Daniel H. Kaiser, *The Laws of Rus'—Tenth to Fifteenth Centuries* (Salt Lake City, UT: C. Schlacks, 1992), 42–43.

9. *Russian Primary Chronicle*, 117, 137.

10. *Russian Primary Chronicle*, 142.

11. Adam of Bremen, *The History of the Archbishops of Hamburg-Bremen*, trans. Francis J. Tschan (New York: Columbia University Press, 2002), 67.

12. *The Chronicle of Novgorod, 1016–1471*, trans. Robert Michell and Nevill Forbes. Camden Third Series, vol. 25 (New York: AMS Press, 1970), 10–11.

CHAPTER 2

1. *The Chronicle of Novgorod, 1016–1471*, trans. Robert Michell and Nevill Forbes (New York: AMS Press, 1970), 66.

2. *The Nikonian Chronicle*, ed. Serge A. Zenkovsky, trans. Serge A. Zenkovsky and Betty Jean Zenkovsky, 5 vols. (Princeton, NJ: Kingston Press, 1984), 2: 312.

3. *The Nikonian Chronicle*, 2: 322.

4. John of Plano Carpini, "History of the Mongols," in *The Mongol Mission*, ed. Christopher Dawson (London: Sheed and Ward, 1955), 15, 65.

5. *Medieval Russia's Epics, Chronicles, and Tales*, ed. Serge Zenkovsky, rev. and enlarged ed. (New York: E. P. Dutton, 1974), 199.

6. *The Chronicle of Novgorod,* 97.

7. "The Journey of William of Rubruck," in *The Mongol Mission,* 157.

8. *The Nikonian Chronicle,* 3: 169–170.

9. *The Nikonian Chronicle,* 3: 105–106.

10. *The Nikonian Chronicle,* 3: 290.

11. *A Source Book for Russian History from Early Times to 1917,* ed. George Vernadsky, 3 vols. (New Haven, CT: Yale University Press, 1972), 1: 56–57.

12. *The Testaments of the Grand Princes of Moscow,* tr. and ed. Robert Craig Howes (Ithaca, NY: Cornell University Press, 1967), 212, 215–216.

13. *The Nikonian Chronicle,* 3: 119.

CHAPTER 3

1. *The Testaments of the Grand Princes of Moscow,* trans. and ed. Robert Craig Howes (Ithaca, NY: Cornell University Press, 1967), 243.

2. Sigismund von Herberstein, *Notes upon Russia,* trans. R. H. Major, Works Issued by the Hakluyt Society, vols. 10 and 12 (London: Hakluyt, 1851; reprint ed. New York: Burt Franklin, n.d.), 10, 96.

3. *Poslaniia Iosifa Volotskogo,* ed. A. A. Zimin and Ya. S. Lur'e (Moscow: Akademiia Nauk SSSR, 1959), 184.

4. von Herberstein, 10: 32.

5. Richard Chancellor, "The First Voyage to Russia," in *Rude and Barbarous Kingdom,* ed. Lloyd E. Berry and Robert O. Crummey (Madison: University of Wisconsin Press, 1968), 18–19.

6. *Dopolneniia k aktam istoricheskim* (Supplement to Historical acts), vol. 1 (St. Petersburg: Arkheograficheskaia kommissiia, 1846), No. 52.28, pp. 109–110.

7. Chancellor, 32.

8. *Dopolneniia k aktam istoricheskim,* No. 126, p. 182.

9. *The Travels of Olearius in Seventeenth-Century Russia,* trans. and ed. Samuel H. Baron (Stanford, CA: Stanford University Press, 1967), 114–115.

10. *Muscovite Judicial Texts, 1488–1556,* ed. and trans. H. W. Dewey (Ann Arbor, MI, 1966), 19.

11. *The Muscovite Law Code (Ulozhenie) of 1649,* trans. and ed. Richard Hellie (Irvine, CA: Charles Schlacks Jr., 1988), chap. 11, article 2, 85, 86.

12. Samuel Collins, *The Present State of Russia in a Letter to a Friend at London* (London, 1671), 65.

13. As quoted by Philip Longworth, *Alexis: Tsar of All the Russias* (New York: Franklin Watts, 1984), 198.

14. As quoted by Lindsey Hughes, *Sophia: Regent of Russia, 1657–1704* (New Haven, CT: Yale University Press, 1990), 190.

15. As quoted by George Heard Hamilton, *The Art and Architecture of Russia* (Harmondsworth, England: Penguin Books, 1974), 170.

16. *The Patriarch and the Tsar. Vol. I: The Replies of the Humble Nicon,* trans. William Palmer (London: Trübner, 1871), 190.

17. As quoted by Paul Avrich, *Russian Rebels, 1600–1800* (New York: W. W. Norton, 1976), 89.

CHAPTER 4

1. *Zapiski Ivana Ivanovicha Nepliueva, 1693–1773.* (1893, repr. Cambridge, MA: Oriental Research Partners, 1974), 103.

2. Johann-Georg Korb, *Diary of an Austrian Secretary at the Court of Czar Peter the Great*, ed. and trans. the Count Mac Donnell, 2 vols. in 1 (New York: Da Capo Press, 1968), 155–156.

3. James Cracraft, ed. *Major Problems in the History of Imperial Russia* (Lexington, MA: D. C. Heath, 1994), 111.

4. Lindsey Hughes, *Russia in the Age of Peter the Great* (New Haven, CT: Yale University Press, 1998), 298.

5. Nepliuev, 56, 73, 76.

6. Korb, 264.

7. Quoted in Daniel Schlafly, "A Muscovite *Boiarynia* Faces Peter the Great's Reforms: Dar'ia Golitsyna between Two Worlds," *Canadian-American Slavic Studies* 31, no. 3 (Fall 1997): 262.

8. Quoted in Hughes, 196.

9. Cracraft, 115.

10. Cracraft, 120.

11. Cracraft, 115.

12. Cracraft, 124.

CHAPTER 5

1. *Days of a Russian Noblewoman. The Memories of Anna Labzina, 1758–1821*, ed. and trans. Gary Marker and Rachel May (DeKalb: Northern Illinois University Press, 2001), 13, 14.

2. *The Memoirs of Princess Dashkova*, ed. and trans. Kyril Fitzlyon, introduction by Jehanne Gheith (Durham, NC: Duke University Press, 1995), 83.

3. Quoted in Peter Kolchin, *Unfree Labor: American Slavery and Russian Serfdom* (Cambridge, MA: Harvard University Press, 1987), 249–250.

4. A. N. Radishchev, *A Journey from St. Petersburg to Moscow*, trans. Leo Wiener, ed. and intro. Roderick Page Thaler, 2nd ed. (Cambridge, MA: Harvard University Press, 1966), 210, 248.

5. *A Life under Russian Serfdom. The Memoirs of Savva Dmitrievich Purlevskii*, ed. and trans. Boris B. Gorshkov (Budapest: Central European University Press, 2005), 97.

6. Quote from Iulia Zhukova, "Pervaia zhenskaia organizatsiia v Rossii (Zhenskoe Patroticheskoe Obshchestvo v Peterburge v period 1812–1826 gg.) in *Vse Liudi Sestry*, Peterburgskii Tsentr Gendernykh Problem, Biulleten' no. 5 (St. Petersburg, 1996), 50.

7. Quote from Sean Pollock, "Petr Ivanovich Bagration (1765–1812)," in *Russia's People of Empire: Life Stories from Eurasia, 1600 to the Present*, ed. Stephen M. Norris and Willard Sunderland (Bloomington: Indiana University Press, 2012), 99.

8. Marc Raeff, ed., *The Decembrist Movement* (Englewood Cliffs, NJ: Prentice-Hall, 1966), 51.

9. Quoted from Mark Bassin, *Imperial Visions: Nationalist Imagination and Geographical Expansion in the Russian Far East, 1840–1865* (Cambridge, UK: Cambridge University Press, 1999), 59.

10. Alexander Herzen, *Childhood, Youth and Exile*, trans. J. D. Duff, with introduction by Isaiah Berlin (New York: Oxford University Press, 1956, 1994), p. 45.

CHAPTER 6

1. Quote, slightly modified, from Jerome Blum, *Lord and Peasant in Russia from the Ninth to the Nineteenth Century* (Princeton, NJ: Princeton University Press, 1961), 578.

2. Quoted in Mark Bassin, *Imperial Visions: Nationalist Imagination and Geographical Expansion in the Russian Far East, 1840–1865* (Cambridge: Cambridge University Press, 1999), 140.

3. Barbara Alpern Engel and Clifford Rosenthal, ed. and trans., *Five Sisters: Women Against the Tsar* (New York: Knopf, 1975), 17.

4. James Cracraft, ed., *Major Problems in the History of Imperial Russia* (Lexington, MA: D. C. Heath, 1994), 390.

5. Quoted in Richard Wortman, *Scenarios of Power: Myth and Ceremony in Russian Monarchy*, 2 vols. (Princeton, NJ: Princeton University Press, 1995–2000), 2: 238.

6. Reginald E. Zelnik, trans. and ed., *A Radical Worker in Tsarist Russia: The Autobiography of Semën Ivanovich Kanatchikov* (Stanford, CA: Stanford University Press, 1986), 6.

7. Robert Weinberg and Laurie Bernstein, ed, *Revolutionary Russia: A History in Documents* (New York: Oxford University Press, 2011), 23–24, 26.

CHAPTER 7

1. http://www.rulit.net/books/rech-p-n-milyukova-na-zasedanii-gosudarstvennoj-dumy-read-105622-4.html.

2. B. Grave, *K istorii klassovoi bor'by v Rossii v gody imperialisticheskoi voiny, iiul' 1914 g.-fevral' 1917 g.* (Moscow: Gos. Izd-vo, 1926), 156–157.

3. Robert Weinberg and Laurie Bernstein, eds., *Revolutionary Russia: A History in Documents* (New York: Oxford University Press, 2011), 53–54.

4. Quoted in Evan Mawdsley, *The Russian Civil War* (Boston: Allen and Unwin, 1987), 143–144.

5. Sheila Fitzpatrick and Yuri Slezkine, eds., *In the Shadow of Revolution: Life Stories of Russian Women from 1917 to the Second World War* (Princeton, NJ: Princeton University Press, 2000), 150.

6. Weinberg and Bernstein, 126.

7. Barbara Alpern Engel and Anastasia Posadskaya-Vanderbeck, eds., *A Revolution of Their Own: Voices of Women in Soviet History* (Boulder, CO: Westview Press, 1998), 32.

8. http://www.soviethistory.org/index.php?page=subject&show=&SubjectID=1936 abortion&ArticleID=&Year=1936.

9. Catherine Merridale, *Ivan's War: Life and Death in the Red Army, 1939–1945* (New York: Picador, 2006), 172.

10. Andrei Sakharov, *Memoirs* (New York: Alfred A. Knopf, 1990), 41.

CHAPTER 8

1. Lev Kopelev, *To Be Preserved Forever,* Anthony Austin, ed. and trans. (Philadelphia: J. B. Lippincott, 1977), 38.

2. Quoted in Archie Brown, *The Rise and Fall of Communism* (New York: HarperCollins, 2009), 176.

3. Mary M. Leder, *My Life in Stalinist Russia: An American Woman Looks Back*, Laurie Bernstein, ed. (Bloomington: Indiana University Press, 2001), 296.

4. http://www.guardian.co.uk/theguardian/2007/apr/26/greatspeeches1.

5. Kim Chernin, *In My Mother's House: A Daughter's Story* (New York: Harper Colophon, 1984), 267.

6. Quoted in Susan E. Reid, "Who Will Beat Whom? Soviet Popular Reception of the American National Exhibition in Moscow," *Kritika: Explorations in Russian and Eurasian History* 9, no. 4 (2008): 891.

7. Quoted in William Taubman, *Khrushchev: The Man and His Era* (New York: W. W. Norton, 2003), 527.

8. Natalya Baranskaya, *A Week like Any Other. Novellas and Stories*, Pieta Monks, trans. (Seattle, WA: Seal Press, 1989), 50.

Further Reading

GENERAL

Blum, Jerome. *Lord and Peasant in Russia, from the Ninth to the Nineteenth Century.* Princeton, NJ: Princeton University Press, 1961.

Gleason, Abbott, ed. *A Companion to Russian History.* Chichester, UK: Wiley-Blackwell, 2009.

Kappeler, Andreas. *The Russian Empire: A Multiethnic History.* Trans. Alfred Clayton. Harlow, UK: Pearson Education, 2001.

Lincoln, W. Bruce. *The Conquest of a Continent: Siberia and the Russians.* New York: Random House, 1994.

Massie, Suzanne. *Land of the Firebird: The Beauty of Old Russia.* New York: Simon and Schuster, 1980.

Norris, Stephen, and Willard Sunderland, eds. *Russia's Peoples of Empire: Life Stories from Eurasia, 1500 to the Present.* Bloomington: Indiana University Press, 2012.

Slezkine, Yuri. *Arctic Mirrors: Russia and the Small Peoples of the North.* Ithaca, NY: Cornell University Press, 1994.

MEDIEVAL AND EARLY MODERN

Barford, P. M. *The Early Slavs: Culture and Society in Early Medieval Eastern Europe.* Ithaca, NY: Cornell University Press, 2001.

Crummey, Robert O. *The Formation of Muscovy, 1304–1613.* London: Longman, 1987.

Dunning, Chester S. L. *Russia's First Civil War: The Time of Troubles and the Founding of the Romanov Dynasty.* University Park: Pennsylvania State University Press, 2001.

Fennell, John. *A History of the Russian Church to 1448.* London: Longman, 1995.

Franklin, Simon. *Writing, Society, and Culture in Early Rus, c. 950–1300.* Cambridge, UK: Cambridge University Press, 2002.

Franklin, Simon, and Jonathan Shepard. *The Emergence of Rus, 750–1200.* London: Longman, 1996.

Hellie, Richard. *Slavery in Russia, 1450–1725.* Chicago: University of Chicago Press, 1982.

Hughes, Lindsey. *Sophia, Regent of Russia, 1657–1704.* New Haven, CT: Yale University Press, 1990.

Kaiser, Daniel H. *The Growth of the Law in Medieval Russia.* Princeton, NJ: Princeton University Press, 1980.

Khodarkovsky, Michael. *Russia's Steppe Frontier: The Making of a Colonial Empire, 1500–1800.* Bloomington: Indiana University Press, 2002.

Kollmann, Nancy Shields. *Crime and Punishment in Early Modern Russia.* New York: Cambridge University Press, 2012.

Martin, Janet. *Medieval Russia, 980–1584*. 2nd ed. Cambridge, UK: Cambridge University Press, 2007.

Michels, Georg Bernhard. *At War with the Church: Religious Dissent in Seventeenth-Century Russia*. Stanford, CA: Stanford University Press, 1999.

Pavlov, Andrei, and Maureen Perrie. *Ivan the Terrible*. Harlow, UK: Pearson Longman, 2003.

Perrie, Maureen, ed. *The Cambridge History of Russia*. Vol. 1, *From Early Rus' to 1689*. Cambridge, UK: Cambridge University Press, 2006.

Raffensperger, Christian. *Reimagining Europe: Kievan Rus' in the Medieval World*. Cambridge, MA: Harvard University Press, 2012.

Romaniello, Matthew P. *The Elusive Empire: Kazan and the Creation of Russia, 1552–1671*. Madison: University of Wisconsin Press, 2012.

Ryan, W. F. *The Bathhouse at Midnight: An Historical Survey of Magic and Divination in Russia*. University Park: Pennsylvania State University Press, 1999.

IMPERIAL RUSSIA

Ascher, Abraham. *The Russian Revolution of 1905: A Short History*. Stanford, CA: Stanford University Press, 2004.

Brooks, Jeffrey. *When Russia Learned to Read: Literacy and Popular Literature, 1861–1917*. Princeton, NJ: Princeton University Press, 1985.

de Madariaga, Isabelle. *Russia in the Age of Catherine the Great*. New Haven, CT: Yale University Press, 1981.

Engel, Barbara Alpern. *Between the Fields and the City: Women, Work and Family in Russia, 1861–1914*. Cambridge, UK: Cambridge University Press, 1994.

Engel, Barbara Alpern, and Clifford Rosenthal, eds. and trans. *Five Sisters: Women against the Tsar*. Rev. ed. DeKalb: Northern Illinois University Press, 2013.

Engelstein, Laura. *The Keys to Happiness: Sex and the Search for Modernity in Fin-de-siècle Russia*. Ithaca, NY: Cornell University Press, 1992.

Hughes, Lindsey. *Russia in the Age of Peter the Great*. New Haven, CT: Yale University Press, 1998.

Hughes, Lindsey. *The Romanovs: Ruling Russia, 1613–1917*. London: Hambledon Continuum, 2008.

Klier, John Doyle. *Russia Gathers Her Jews: The Origins of the Jewish Question in Russia*. DeKalb: Northern Illinois University Press, 1986.

Lieven, Dominic, ed. *Cambridge History of Russia*. Vol. 2, *Imperial Russia, 1689–1917*. Cambridge, UK: Cambridge University Press, 2006.

Lincoln, W. Bruce. *Passage through Armageddon: The Russians in War and Revolution*. New York: Simon and Schuster, 1986.

Marrese, Michelle LaMarche. *A Woman's Kingdom: Noblewomen and the Control of Property in Russia, 1700–1861*. Ithaca, NY: Cornell University Press, 2002.

Moon, David. *The Russian Peasantry, 1600–1930: The World the Peasants Made*. London: Longman, 1999.

Smith, Douglas. *The Pearl: A True Tale of Forbidden Love in Catherine the Great's Russia*. New Haven, CT: Yale University Press, 2008.

Steinberg, Mark D., and Heather J. Coleman, eds. *Sacred Stories: Religion and Spirituality in Modern Russia*. Bloomington: Indiana University Press, 2007.

Sunderland, Willard. *Taming the Wild Field: Colonization and Empire on the Russian Steppe*. Ithaca, NY: Cornell University Press, 2004.

Barber, John, and Mark Harrison. *The Soviet Home Front: 1941–1945.* London: Longman, 1991.

David-Fox, Michael. *Showcasing the Great Experiment: Cultural Diplomacy and Western Visitors to the Soviet Union, 1921–1941.* New York: Oxford University Press, 2012.

Engel, Barbara, and Anastasia Posadskaya-Vanderbeck. *A Revolution of Their Own: Voices of Women in Soviet History.* Boulder, CO: Westview Press, 1997.

Figes, Orlando. *The Whisperers: Private Life in Stalin's Russia.* New York: Metropolitan Books, 2007.

Fitzpatrick, Sheila. *Stalin's Peasants: Resistance and Survival in the Russian Village after Collectivization.* New York: Oxford University Press, 1994.

Gessen, Masha. *The Man without a Face: The Unlikely Rise of Vladimir Putin.* New York: Riverhead Books, 2013.

Ginzburg, Eugenia S. *Journey into the Whirlwind.* Trans. Paul Stevenson and Max Hayward. San Diego: Harcourt Brace, 1967.

Gorsuch, Anne. *All This Is Your World: Soviet Tourism at Home and Abroad after Stalin.* New York: Oxford University Press, 2011.

Kotkin, Stephen. *Magnetic Mountain: Stalinism as a Civilization.* Berkeley: University of California Press, 1995.

Martin, Terry. *The Affirmative Action Empire: Nations and Nationalism in the Soviet Union, 1923–1939.* Ithaca, NY: Cornell University Press, 2001.

Overy, Richard. *Russia's War: A History of the Soviet War Effort, 1941–1945.* New York: Penguin, 1998.

Pasternak, Boris. *Doctor Zhivago.* New York: Penguin, 2010.

Plokhii, Serhii. *The Last Empire: The Final Days of the Soviet Union.* New York: Basic Books, 2014.

Raleigh, Donald. *Soviet Baby Boomers: An Oral History of Russia's Cold War Generation.* New York: Oxford University Press, 2011.

Steinberg, Mark D., and Vladimir M. Khrustalev. *The Fall of the Romanovs: Political Dreams and Personal Struggles in a Time of Revolution.* New Haven, CT: Yale University Press, 1995.

Suny, Ronald Grigor, ed. *Cambridge History of Russia.* Vol. 3, *The Twentieth Century.* Cambridge, UK: Cambridge University Press, 2006.

Taubman, William. *Khrushchev: The Man and His Era.* New York: Norton, 2003.

Tumarkin, Nina. *Lenin Lives: The Lenin Cult in Soviet Russia.* 2nd ed. Cambridge, MA: Harvard University Press, 1997.

Wade, Rex A. *The Russian Revolution, 1917.* Cambridge, UK: Cambridge University Press, 2000.

Websites

Art and Architecture of Novgorod
www.novgorod.ru/english/
 The website of the city of Novgorod is a rich source on icons and icon-painting, ancient Rus architecture, and Russian Orthodox hymnody.

The Cold War
http://digitalarchive.wilsoncenter.org/theme/cold-war-history
 The Cold War International History Project offers an enormous collection of archival documents from the Cold War era, drawn from once-secret archives of formerly communist states.

Documents from Soviet Archives
www.ibiblio.org/expo/soviet.exhibit/soviet.archive.html
 The Library of Congress makes available a wide-ranging selection of archival documents, many of them once secret, from the early days of Soviet rule through Perestroika.

Everyday Life in the Soviet Union
http://kommunalka.colgate.edu/cfm/about.cfm
 Visit a communal apartment and learn about everyday life in the Soviet Union from interviews, historical documents, film, photographs and more.

The Gulag, or Concentration Camp System
http://gulaghistory.org/
 A project of the Roy Rozenzweig Center for History and New Media at George Mason University presents an in-depth look at life in the Soviet concentration camp system.

The Hermitage Museum
www.hermitagemuseum.org/html_En/03/hm3_6.html
 Among the holdings in the magnificent art collection at the Hermitage Museum are archeological artifacts, icons, and secular art from the imperial era. The site also provides narrative descriptions and information about the artwork.

Jews of Russia and the Soviet Union
www.friends-partners.org/partners/beyond-the-pale/english/guide-cond.html
 A narrative history of Russia's Jews, accompanied by illustrations and photographs.

The Last of the Romanovs
www.alexanderpalace.org/palace/mainpage.html
 Browse materials concerning the last Romanov family, including photographs, biographies of key figures, eye-witness accounts, and contemporary newspapers reports.

Photographs of Russian Historic Sites
www.loc.gov/pictures/collection/brum
 William Brumfield's collection of photographs, housed in the Library of Congress, contains images of historic sites throughout Russia, many only recently accessible to foreign visitors.

Photographs of the Russian empire
www.loc.gov/exhibits/empire/
 The photographs taken by Sergei Prokudin-Gorskii, a pioneering color photographer who ranged all over the empire, offer a vivid photographic portrait of the final decades of imperial Russia.

Radio Free Europe

www.rferl.org/section/russia/161.html
Radio Free Europe offers up-to-date news on Russia, with links to in-depth analyses, photographs, and historical materials.

Russian Cultural History

www.pbs.org/weta/faceofrussia/
From the Public Broadcasting Series on Russian cultural history, with links to images, movies and audio tracks, covering the earliest days of Russia's history through 2000.

Russians in Alaska

www.loc.gov/exhibits/russian/s1a.html
A site devoted to the history of Russians in Alaska, which continued even after Alaska was sold to the United States in 1867. It includes archival documents, maps and photographs.

Soviet History Online

www.soviethistory.org/index.php
A wealth of photographs, images, videos, maps, and music, and other primary sources drawn from the entirety of Soviet history, and including scholarly essays on key historical moments, arranged by year and subject.

The Tretyakov Gallery

www.tretyakovgallery.ru/en/collection
The collection of the Tretyakov Gallery in Moscow includes works by Russian artists from the 12th century through modern times.

Acknowledgments

For their assistance with the illustrations for this book, we are grateful to the State Hermitage Museum, St. Petersburg, the Tretyakov Gallery, Alexei Gippius, and Magdalena Stawkowski. Our warm thanks to Bonnie Smith and Anand Yang for inviting us to undertake this project, to Nancy Toff, for her astute editorial guidance along the way, to Rebecca Hecht for assistance with matters large and small, and to the anonymous readers of our manuscript for their discerning observations and helpful comments.

NEW OXFORD WORLD
HISTORY

The
New
Oxford
World
History

GENERAL EDITORS

BONNIE G. SMITH,
Rutgers University
ANAND A. YANG,
University of Washington

EDITORIAL BOARD

DONNA GUY,
Ohio State University
KAREN ORDAHL KUPPERMAN,
New York University
MARGARET STROBEL,
University of Illinois, Chicago
JOHN O. VOLL,
Georgetown University

The New Oxford World History
provides a comprehensive,
synthetic treatment of the
"new world history" from
chronological, thematic, and
geographical perspectives,
allowing readers to access the
world's complex history from a
variety of conceptual, narrative,
and analytical viewpoints as it fits
their interests.

Barbara Alpern Engel is
Distinguished Professor of History
at the University of Colorado,
Boulder. She is the author of
*Mothers and Daughters: Women
of the Intelligentsia in Nineteenth
Century Russia* (1983), *Between
the Fields and the City: Women,
Work and Family in Russia* (1994),
Women in Russia: 1700–2000
(2004), and *Breaking the Ties that
Bound: The Politics of Marital
Strife in Late Imperial Russia*
(2011), as well as numerous
articles. She is co-editor of
*Five Sisters: Women Against
the Tsar* (1975), *Russia's
Women: Accommodation,
Resistance, Transformation*
(1991), and *A Revolution of Their
Own: Russian Women Remember
their Lives in the Twentieth
Century* (1998).

Janet Martin is Professor Emerita of
History at the University of Miami.
She is the author of *Treasure of the
Land of Darkness: the Fur Trade
and its Significance for Medieval
Russia* (1986) and *Medieval Russia,
980-1584* (1995), as well as dozens
of articles.

Index

emancipation of serfs. *See* serfdom
epidemics, 12, 20, 22, 100
Estonia, 102, 107, 110, 113, 115,
    122–123, 124
Ethiopia, 121
ethnic minorities
    policies towards, 31, 36, 38, 44, 63, 65,
        99, 124
    religious conversion of, 31
    taxation of, 38, 44
    unrest among, 44, 60, 65, 93, 94,
        96, 99
    See also Communist Party, national
        minorities and; Russification
Eugene Onegin, 72
Europe
    competition with, 45–46, 75
    dependence on, 47
    diplomatic missions to, 58
    Russia's stature in, 58, 61, 70, 73, 74
    See also foreign influence, European;
        trade, foreign

family life, 33, 87
famines, 12, 20, 86, 88, 101, 103, 110
Fathers and Children, 78
February Revolution, 94–95
Feodor Ivanovich, Tsar, 38
Ferghana Valley, 86, 103
Figner, Vera, 79
Filosofova, Anna, 76
Finland, 81, 102
Finns, viii, x, 1, 2, 4, 6, 7, 9, 21
Fioravanti, Aristotele, 28, 30, 32
First Five Year Plan, 104
food dictatorship, 100
forced labor, 103, 104, 107, 108
foreign influence, 120, 119
    Byzantine, 1, 7, 8–9, 13, 26, 29
    European, 29, 32, 40, 41–42, 48, 50,
        51–52, 54, 56, 63, 76
    French, 70
    Hollywood, 106
    Mongol, 20–21, 27
    resistance to, 7, 42–43, 56–57, 66,
        71–72, 80, 112, 126
foreign intervention, 99
foreign investment, 82, 104
France, 8, 9, 74, 75, 84, 92, 99
    in War of 1812, 69, 70
French Revolution of 1789, 66

Gagarin, Yurii, 116
Gandhi, Mahatma, xi
gender relations, 76
gendered imagery, 61
Georgia, 99, 123, 124
German quarter, 42, 49
Germany, 75, 84, 101, 107, 122

threat of, 111
    in World War I, 92
    in World War II, 107–109
    See also World War I; World War II
glasnost', 121, 122
Golden Horde, 23, 25
    commerce of, 20, 22
    disintegration of the, 22, 24, 27, 30, 31
    establishment of the, 15
    and Russian Orthodox Church, 17, 18
    Tatar Yoke, end of the, 31
    tribute collection by, 18, 21–22, 27
    See also Mongols; Sarai
gold standard, 82
Golitsyn, Prince Vasilii, 42
Gorbachev, Mikhail, vii, 121–122, 124
Great Britain, 69, 70, 74, 75, 84, 92,
    99, 109
Great Depression, 104
Great Horde, 24, 31
Great Reforms, 77–78
Guards regiments, 49, 61, 66

health care, 42, 78, 112, 120
Herberstein, Sigismund von, 31–32, 33
Hermogen, Patriarch 38. *See also* Time of
    Troubles
Herzen, Aleksandr, 71, 73, 79
Hiroshima, atomic bombing of, 111, 123
Hitler, Adolph, 102, 106, 108
Hoover, Herbert, 101
Hungary, viii, 1, 8, 14, 16, 101, 115

Ibn Fadlan, 4
icons, 9, 19, 26, 40, 42
    "Old Testament Trinity", 26
    "Our Lady of Vladmir", 13
    and portraiture, 43
Igor, Prince of Kiev. *See* Olga, Princess.
industrialization, 68, 82, 102–103, 104,
    105, 112, 115
    of warfare, 93
    and World War II, 108–109
    See also economic development;
        manufacturing
infantrymen, 40
Iona, Bishop of Ryazan and
    Metropolitan, 27
iron curtain, 111
Isidor, Metropolitan, 26–27
Islam, 7, 31, 86
Italy, 70, 107
    Ferrara-Florence, Council of, 26–27
Ivan I Kalita, Grand Prince of Vladimir,
    21, 22, 25
Ivan III, Grand Prince, 28, 29–33
Ivan IV the Terrible, Tsar, 30, 32,
    33–36, 38, 41
Ivan V, Tsar, 42, 48

and secularization of lands, 56
  See also Ecclesiastic Regulations;
    individual metropolitans and
    patriarchs by name
Russian Social Democratic Labor
  Party, 88
Russification, 81, 84
Russo-Japanese War, 84, 88–89, 90
Ryazan, 16, 18, 21, 24, 25
Ryurik, 1, 4
Ryurikid dynasty, 6, 7, 12, 17, 20, 38
  succession system, 11, 21, 27

Sakharov, Andrei, 109, 119–120, 122
Salisbury, Harrison, 112
Samarkand, 85
Sarai, 17, 18, 22, 24
science and technology, 42, 48, 51, 77, 82,
  113, 116, 119
scientific revolution, 48
scorched earth, 68
Semeon Ivanovich, Grand Prince, 20
serfdom
  abolition of, 75–77
  as brake on economic
    development, 68, 75
  critique of, 66, 70
  establishment of, 40–41
  intensification of, 64
  See also serfs; peasants
serfs
  emancipation of, 67, 75–77
  as entertainers, 64
  entrepreneurism of, 67–68
  merchants and, 54
  and the military, 53
  resistance of, 65, 75
Sergei of Radonezh, 25–26, 27
settlers, 36, 60, 65, 84–85
Shamil, Imam, 72
"shock therapy," 126
Siberia, 15, 34, 84, 99, 126
  peoples of, x, 36, 38, 103
  Russian conquest of, ix, 36, 38
Siege of Leningrad, 107
Silk Road. *See* Golden Horde,
  commerce of
Sipyagin, Dmitrii, 88
Sit River, Battle of, 16
slavery, 4, 5, 7, 10, 11, 18, 32, 35, 36, 64
Slavic Greek Latin Academy, 64
Slavophiles, 73
Slavs, viii, x, 1, 3–6, 7, 8, 9
Smolensk, 10, 11, 14, 31, 40
Smolny Institute for Girls of Noble
  Birth, 64
sobornost', 73
socialism, 73, 79, 87, 92–93, 97.
Socialism in One Country, 102

socialist realism, 106
Socialist Revolutionary Party, 88
Solzhenitsyn, Alexander, 118
Sophia Alekseevna, 42, 49
Sophia (Zoë) Palaeologa, 29
Soviet Union, *See* Union of Soviet Socialist
  Republics
soviets, 97. *See also* Petrograd Soviet
Spain, 70, 107
Speransky, Mikhail, 67
Sputnik, 116
St. Petersburg, 56, 57, 86, 94–95, 99, 107
Stakhanovite movement, 105
Stalin, Joseph, 102–103, 107, 110, 113,
  115, 118
  Cold War and, 111, 112
  criticism of, 115, 118, 119, 121
  cult of, 106, 109, 114
  terror and, 106, 107, 113, 115
  See also Communist Party
Stalingrad, Battle of, 108
Stasova, Nadezhda, 76
Stenka Razin rebellion, 44
steppe, viii–ix, 3, 5, 12, 15
  Mongol control over, 16, 17
  nomads, x, 1, 5, 6, 14, 15, 47, 65, 85,
    103 (*see also* Nogai; Pechenegs;
    Qïpchaqs; Tatars)
strikes, 87, 89, 90–91, 93, 94, 94–95
Stroganov family, 36
superfluous men, 72
Suzdalia (Vladimir-Suzdal), 11, 13, 17,
  19, 20, 21, 22, 24 (*see also* Vladimir
  (city))
Sweden, ix, 4, 8, 34–35, 46, 49, 52, 55, 69

Table of Ranks, 54
*Tale of Bygone Years. See Primary
  Chronicle*
Tashkent, 84
Tatars, 16, 18, 21, 23–24, 25, 28,
  31, 32, 36
  Crimean, 34–35, 63, 108
  See also Crimean Khanate; Kazan,
    Khanate of; Mongols
Tereshkova, Valentina, 116
Terror of 1936–38, 106–107, 115, 119
terrorism, 114. *See also* Red Terror
Teutonic Knights, Order of, 14
Thaw, The, 114
Theodore Roosevelt, US President, 90
Theophanes the Greek, 19
Third Section, 72
Thirteen Years' War, 40, 41, 44
Tilsit, Treaty of, 69
Time of Troubles, 38, 39, 40
Timur, 24
Tolstoy, Leo, xi, 68–69
Toqtamïsh, 22, 24